STUDENT AFFAIRS ASSESSMENT, EVALUATION, AND RESEARCH

Publication Number 1

AMERICAN SERIES IN STUDENT AFFAIRS
PRACTICE AND PROFESSIONAL IDENTITY

Edited by

NAIJIAN ZHANG, PH.D.

West Chester University
Department of Counselor Education
West Chester, PA

STUDENT AFFAIRS ASSESSMENT, EVALUATION, AND RESEARCH

A Guidebook for Graduate Students and New Professionals

Edited by

VICKI L. WISE, PH.D.

and

ZEBULUN R. DAVENPORT, ED.D.

Foreword by Naijian Zhang

(With 13 Other Contributors)

CHARLES C THOMAS · PUBLISHER · LTD.
Springfield · Illinois · U.S.A.

Published and Distributed Throughout the World by

CHARLES C THOMAS • PUBLISHER, LTD.
2600 South First Street
Springfield, Illinois 62704

© 2019 by CHARLES C THOMAS • PUBLISHER, LTD.

ISBN 978-0-398-09263-4 (paper)
ISBN 978-0-398-09264-1 (ebook)

Library of Congress Catalog Card Number: 2018055103

Printed in the United States of America
MM-C-1

Library of Congress Cataloging-in-Publication Data

Names: Wise, Vicki L., editor. | Davenport, Zebulun R., editor. |
   Zhang, Naijian, writer of foreword.
Title: Student affairs assessment, evaluation, and research : a guide-
   book for graduate students and new professionals / edited by Vicki
   L. Wise and Zebulun Davenport ; foreword by Naijian Zhang.
Description: Springfield, Illinois : Charles C Thomas, Publisher, Ltd.,
   [2019] | Series: American series in student affairs practice and pro-
   fessional identity | Includes bibliographical references and index.
Identifiers: LCCN 2018055103 (print) | LCCN 2019000184 (ebook) |
   ISBN 9780398092641 (ebook) | ISBN 9780398092634 (paper)
Subjects: LCSH: Student affairs services—United States.
Classification: LCC LB2342.92 (ebook) | LCC LB2342.92 .S77 2019
   (print) | DDC 371.40973—dc23
LC record available at https://lccn.loc.gov/2018055103

FOREWORD

Assessment is today's means of modifying tomorrow's instruction.
Carol Ann Tomlinson

*S*tudent Affairs Assessment, Evaluation, and Research: A Guidebook for Graduate
Students and New Professionals *is a valuable tool for all student affairs educators. While this book is designed for those who are preparing to become student affairs educators and for those who are new to this discipline, it is certainly filled with information and resources for entry-level, mid-level, and senior-level professionals. This book is not only a blueprint but also a global positioning system on assessment, evaluation, and research in student affairs to guide you in the process of helping and educating students on the American college and university campus in the twenty-first century. Furthermore, this book is a bridge that connects between who you are today and who you want to be as a student affairs educator tomorrow. It will help you operationalize your goal to become a competent practitioner in the area of assessment, evaluation, and research in student affairs of higher education. It is a unique and valuable source to develop your professional competency.*

Student Affairs Assessment, Evaluation, and Research: A Guidebook for Graduate Students and New Professionals is an essential volume in the *American Series in Student Affairs Practice and Professional Identity in the 21st Century*. The significance of this book is due to its focus on the practical value of assessment, evaluation, and research, a professional competency area for student affairs educators articulated by ACPA/NASPA in both 2010 and 2015. This book has aimed to have a complete reflection of this competency area.

The core value of *Student Affairs Assessment, Evaluation, and Research: A Guidebook for Graduate Students and New Professionals* is the organized knowledge and organized experiences or wisdoms in assessment, evaluation, and research from both the editors and all the chapter authors. The editors of the book, Dr. Vicki L. Wise and Dr. Zebulun Davenport, are true scientists and practitioners in the field of student affairs in higher education. Playing critical roles in assessment, evaluation, and research at different higher education institutions, they have gained numerous years of hands-on experiences through the integration of their knowledge into practice. As experts in student affairs of higher education, Dr. Wise and Dr. Davenport have identified high quality practitioners and scholars in assessment, evaluation, and research from colleges and universities and higher-education industry and completed this book project. These authors all hold senior-level positions, and together as a team have enriched this book with their precious knowledge and experiences and now present it as a gift to you—the future and new student affairs educators.

This book has another unique dimension in that it assists you to learn how to develop your professional competency and achieve the foundational, intermediate, and advanced outcomes as identified by ACPA/NASPA. Specifically, it first helps you develop your ability to understand and differentiate among assessment, evaluation, and research. Second, the book helps you learn how to design, conduct, and critique AER. Third, the text guides you to develop competency in appropriate data collection and data analysis. Fourth, the book aids you to foster your professional competency in correct data interpreting, reporting, and using results.

Student Affairs Assessment, Evaluation, and Research: A Guidebook for Graduate Students and New Professionals' next unique dimension is that it facilitates you to learn the value of assessment and the ethical principles associated with assessment and evaluation. Student affairs educators must adhere to the profession's ethical standards and follow the institution's policies and procedures. As being said, future and new student affairs educators must be cognizant of the political, cultural, and social aspects of assessment, evaluation, and research. The book provides you with the tools to develop your professional competency as leaders in the student affairs profession.

Its final unique dimension is that it has accurately reflected the three themes of the *American Series in Student Affairs Practice and Professional Identity in the 21st Century*—professional competencies, professional identity, and application. To accomplish this goal, Dr. Wise and Dr. Davenport with all other chapter authors have skillfully woven the assessment, evaluation, and research (AER) competency into student affairs educators' professional identity. The book provides graduate students in student affairs programs and new student affairs educators with not only why professional identity is important in assessment, evaluation, and research but also knowledge and skills in how to build their professional identity with the competency in practice.

The *American Series in Student Affairs Practice and Professional Identity in the 21st Century* is a unique book series that creates an integration of all ten professional competency areas for student affairs educators outlined by the College Student Educators International (ACPA) and the Student Affairs Administrators in Higher Education (NASPA) in 2015. The series reflects three major themes: professional competencies development, professional identity construction, and case illustrations for theory translation into application. All volumes in the series are targeting graduate students in student affairs programs and new student affairs educators. The series blends contemporary theory with current research and empirical support and uses case illustrations to facilitate the readers' ability to translate what they have learned into application and decision making. Each volume focuses on one area of professional competency and at the same time addresses some major aspects of the Interaction of Competencies. The series helps graduate students in student affairs programs and new student affairs educators develop their professional competencies (ACPA/NASPA) by (1) constructing their personal and ethical foundations; (2) understanding the values, philosophy, and history of student affairs; (3) strengthening their ability in assessment, evaluation, and research; (4) gaining knowledge, skills, and dispositions relating to law, policy, and governance; (5) familiarizing with and learning how to effectively utilize organizational and human resources; (6) learning leadership knowledge and developing leadership skills; (7) understanding oppression, privilege, power, and then learning how to understand social justice and apply it in practice; (8) acquiring student development theories and learning how to use them to inform their practice; (9) familiarizing themselves with technologies and implementing digital means and resources into practice; and (10) gaining advising and supporting knowledge, skills, and dispositions. As a result, the series helps graduate students in student affairs programs and new student affairs educators foster their professional identity and ultimately achieve their goal of the whole-person education.

Naijian Zhang, Ph.D.

PREFACE

This book is a part of the American Series in Student Affairs Practice and Professional Identity in the Twenty-First Century. The series exposes graduate students and new professionals to the professional competency of Assessment, Evaluation, and Research in student affairs as articulated in the ACPA and NASPA *Professional Competency Areas for Student Affairs Educators* (American College Personnel Association & National Association of Student Personnel Administrators, 2015). Assessment, Evaluation, and Research (AER) is one of the 10 professional competency areas identified for student affairs educators. The professional competency areas lay out essential knowledge, skills, and dispositions expected of all student affairs educators, regardless of functional area or specialization within the field (p. 7). The focus throughout this book is developing a professional practice and identity based on the values, philosophy, and history of the profession. In keeping with the theme of the series, this book emphasizes professional competency, professional identity, and application.

Never before in the history of this discipline has it been more important for student affairs professionals to obtain the skills and competencies necessary to assess their programs and services and share their findings with invested audiences. For several valid reasons, the expectations for assessment, evaluation, and research have increased. These factors include, but are not limited to, increased costs of education (i.e., tuition and fees), diminished funding from federal and state agencies, increased budget cuts on college campuses, increased scrutiny for accountability and quality by accrediting bodies, and questioning from parents and students about the worth of a college degree for career preparation and employment given the costs associated with obtaining said degree.

Moreover, increased demand for evidence of success of high-impact practices (HIPS) and cocurricular high-impact practices (CHIPS) continues to rise. Thus, it is vital that student affairs professionals learn the value of AER early in their careers. Cocurricular experiences is an area in which student affairs makes relevant contributions and uniquely completes the educational mission of the college experience. Therefore, understanding the value of high-quality cocurricular programs, continuous improvement, and the need to validate learning outside of the classroom are necessary for all student affairs professionals. In fact, AER should be a mandatory component of every higher education in student affairs (HESA) program in the country.

This book provides the reader with a unique approach to learning and understanding AER. It is designed in a format that describes/defines this competency at the foundational, intermediate, and advanced outcomes levels; suggests ways to apply this competency in practice through case studies from student affairs; and provides tools for assessment of competency understanding.

Book Overview

This book opens with an exploration of the history of assessment in higher education, in general, and then student affairs, more specifically. Having established a historical perspective, the reader then delves into chapters that align with the Assessment, Evaluation, and Research (AER) competency and accompanying rubric (American College Personnel Association & National Association of Student Personnel Administrators, 2016). Chapters 2–8 also include relevant terminology necessary for understanding, the competency applied to a case study, and an opportunity for self-assessment.

Chapter 1, "The Status of Assessment, Evaluation, and Research in Student Affairs," provides the framework for the status of AER though a glance into seminal publications that have shaped this competency. The importance of and attention to assessment, evaluation, and research in higher education is not a recent phenomenon. Contemporary discussions and guidance regarding AER are firmly rooted in the contributions and insights of professionals who long preceded us. The authors close this chapter with a discussion of the role of higher education and student affairs (HESA) graduate programs in building capacity in AER. Presenting this background information sets the stage for addressing and applying AER competency.

Chapter 2, "The Development of Competencies in Assessment, Evaluation, and Research," with Terms and Concepts," explores the history of the Professional Competency Areas for student affairs educators, in general, and the AER competency, more specifically. Readers examine AER at the three levels of outcomes— foundational, intermediate, and advanced— as well as their aligned rubrics. The author provides definitions for relevant terms and concepts associated with assessment, program review, evaluation, planning, and research, as well as terms presented in subsequent chapters for readers to explore. Understanding and applying AER terminology is essential for one's own AER professional development.

Chapter 3, "Student Affairs Assessment in the Broader Institutional Context: Values, Ethics, and Politics," examines the value of assessment and the ethical principles associated with data collection, management, analysis, and reporting. The need to understand and follow institutional policies and procedures, to adhere to standards, and to navigate institutional politics effectively is essential to sustain a culture of assessment that uses results for continuous improvement. The reader is asked to develop an ability to connect the concepts of data and information literacy, data quality, and data use; to identify the roles of transparency and political nuance; to understand the necessity of collaboration and attention to the needs of stakeholders; and the necessity of developing a culture of evidence.

Chapter 4, "Assessment, Evaluation, and Research Design," underscores the importance of having theoretical frameworks that align with organizational outcomes, goals, and values. This chapter examines the ability to create learner-centered outcomes that align with divisional and institutional priorities, and to design and lead a process-oriented strategy to address the assessment's purpose or research questions. The reader is asked to develop an aptitude to think critically and systematically about questions and problems of quality assessment practice. By engaging in an outcomes-based approach, intentional processes and strategies, and a disposition to evidence-based, data-informed work, the reader will master and advance through AER design competency.

Chapter 5, "Methodology, Data Collection, and Data Analysis," informs the reader of the strengths and limits of research methodologies. The ability to match methodology with purpose of assessment and guiding questions and to collect and analyze data are essential to quality AER practice, as is understanding issues of reliability and validity. Readers are implored to take a critical stance in collecting and analyzing data with rigorous attention to detail, and as they apply this competency, to develop these two habits of practice. One, plan as much as possible. Strive to begin with the context, goals, and research questions of your AER effort, and then align the methodology and data collection that best meets those demands. Second, rely on the expertise of others through engagement in collaborations and resource use to advance your AER efforts. These habits are valuable guides to expand your own understanding and skills.

Chapter 6, "Interpreting, Reporting, and Using Results," encourages the reader to explore how to interpret data in practical terms that are relevant to the institutional context, to present results concisely in reports that are useful to a variety of audiences, and to use findings to make informed decisions and to align resources. In particular, this chapter focuses on interpreting data, reporting findings, and utilizing results in ways that support learning in cocurricular programs. Knowing how to interpret and present data in ways that communicate a story is critical to the work of student affairs professionals. Readers will be exposed to skills and techniques that will assist in their development to collaborate, to represent findings accurately and fairly, and to share interpretations with stakeholders, including students.

Chapter 7, "The Role of Assessment, Evaluation, and Research in Professional Development and Professional Identity," encourages the reader to become actively engaged in service and leadership within the profession on many levels including involvement with professional associations. Assessment, evaluation, and research play a significant role in the identity and career development of all student affairs professionals. Therefore, readers are encouraged to keep AER central to their professional identity. This chapter encourages readers to participate in opportunities to identify and incorporate emerging values of the profession into their professional practice. The assessment, evaluation, and research framework can also guide areas of needed professional skill development, which can advance assessment practice at the departmental or divisional levels.

Chapter 8, "The Scholarship of Assessment, Evaluation, and Research in Student Affairs," implores the reader to think of the practice of AER alongside the practice of scholarship. Readers are encouraged to actualize AER by collaborating with faculty and staff for teaching, research, and scholarship regarding the profession; and by contributing to the research, scholarship, and expansion of knowledge within the profession. The authors provide a four-step process for the reader to learn, engage, and develop a scholar-practitioner approach to this discipline.

ABOUT THE EDITORS, CONTRIBUTORS, AND REVIEWERS

About the Editors

Vicki L. Wise, Ph.D., is the Director of Assessment and Accreditation in the College of Public Health and Human Sciences at Oregon State University. In her previous role as Associate Director for Teaching, Learning, and Assessment, she was instrumental in leading Portland State University (PSU) into a new era of quality assessment practice and accountability by integrating assessment processes across levels from the course to the program to the institution. Previously, at PSU, she served as Director of Student Affairs Assessment & Research. Prior to PSU, she held the positions of Director of Assessment and Evaluation for the College of Education, Assistant Director for Institutional Research, and Assistant Professor/Research Administrator in the Center for Assessment and Research Studies, all at James Madison University. She earned her Ph.D. and M.A. degrees at the University of Nebraska in Psychological and Cultural Studies and Educational Psychology, respectively. Her research interests and publications are in the area of applied assessment practice in higher education.

Zebulun R. Davenport, Ed.D., is the Vice President for Student Affairs at West Chester University. He earned his Doctorate in Higher Education and Leadership from Nova Southeastern University, a Master of Education in College Student Personnel Administration, and a Bachelor of Science in Communications/Public Relations with a minor in Human Services from James Madison University. His contributions have advanced campus culture, organizational structure, and student success. His expertise includes the areas of student retention, outcomes assessment, strategic planning, and strategies for assisting first-generation college students. Zeb's publications include co-authoring a book entitled *First-Generation College Students—Understanding and Improving the Experience from Recruitment to Commencement;* a chapter in an edited volume entitled *The Student Success Conundrum,* in B. Bontrager (Ed.), *Strategic Enrollment Management: Transforming Higher Education;* and a chapter in an edited monograph entitled *Creating Collaborative Conditions for Student Success* in S. Whalen (Ed.), *Proceedings of the 8th National Symposium on Student Retention 2012*. He has presented at workshops for numerous public agencies; educational institutions; state, regional, and national conferences; as well as to thousands of college students and professionals throughout his career.

About the Contributors

R. Lorraine Bernotsky, D.Phil., is the Executive Vice President for Academic Affairs and Provost at West Chester University (WCU) of Pennsylvania. Prior to assuming this role, Dr. Bernotsky served as Associate Provost and Dean of Graduate Studies at WCU, providing leadership in the areas of curriculum development, general education, new program development, program review, assessment, regional and specialized external accreditation, articulation agreements with other two- and four-year institutions, academic policies, and faculty development. During the past two years, she led the approval of WCU's first three doctoral programs, the Doctor of Nursing Practice, the Doctor of Public Administration, and a Doctor of Education, as well as four new master's degree programs. She has also reversed the decline in graduate enrollments, moving from a projected decline of 16.94 percent in fall 2013 to an increase of more than 9 percent over the last three years. Dr. Bernotsky is also the founder of WCU's Center for Social and Economic Policy Research. As the Center's founder and first director, her efforts in development yielded over $3 million in funding from state, foundation, corporate, and nonprofit sources to sustain the Center's research activities. Dr. Bernotsky earned an M.Phil. and a D.Phil. in Politics from the University of Oxford and an M.A. in Sociology from Temple University.

Sara J. Finney, Ph.D., is an Associate Director in the Center for Assessment & Research Studies, and a Professor in the Department of Graduate Psychology, both at James Madison University. Since 2001, Dr. Finney has been providing outcomes assessment-related support to professionals in the Division of Student Affairs at James Madison University. Most recently, she has overseen the creation of initiatives to emphasize the use of assessment results for learning improvement. Dr. Finney's work evaluating the effectiveness of university educational programming has garnered four national awards from the American College Personnel Association (ACPA) and the Student Affairs Administrators in Higher Education Association (NASPA). Dr. Finney has published over 55 articles and chapters, with her students co-authoring over 70 percent of these publications. Her research involves the study of test-taking motivation and emotions during institutional accountability testing, the incorporation of implementation fidelity assessment during the outcomes assessment process, and the application of latent variable modeling techniques to better understand the measurement of psychoeducational constructs.

Martha Glass, Ph.D., is the Senior Director of Assessment and Professional Development at Virginia Tech. Martha coordinates assessment for 23 departments to develop and implement outcomes-based assessment strategies including comprehensive program reviews, that lead to continuous improvement of programs and services that support student learning. She also assists with strategic planning and accreditation activities, and she serves in a leadership role in developing a cocurricular experience for students around division-wide learning goals. Dr. Glass holds a Ph.D. in Educational Leadership and Policy Studies in Higher Education from Virginia Tech. She is also an affiliated faculty member in the Higher Education program at Virginia Tech. She created two courses focused on assessment in higher education. Martha serves on the board of the ACPA Commission on Assessment and Evaluation and is a member of the ACPA/NASPA Rubric Task Force for professional competencies. She was the chair for the 2017 ACPA Assessment Institute.

Lisa J. Hatfield, Ed.D., is the Director of Assessment & Evaluation at Oregon Health & Science University–Portland State University School of Public Health. In her previous experience, Lisa was Director of Learning Center, Portland State University; and adjunct faculty for the Lewis & Clark graduate program in Student Affairs Administration. Her research interests are in the areas of fostering scholarly writing and P-20 education.

S. Jeanne Horst, Ph.D. is an Associate Professor and Associate Assessment Specialist in the Center for Assessment and Research Studies at James Madison University. Jeanne provides assessment consultation for a variety of programs across the James Madison University campus. She has worked with numerous student affairs programs, including service learning, multicultural student services, and international programs. Her student affairs-related publications are in the domains of scale development of attitudinal measures and the application of a mixed methods approach to evaluating student learning.

Lance Kennedy-Phillips, Ph.D., is the Vice Provost for Planning and Assessment at Penn State University. As vice provost, Kennedy-Phillips is responsible for leading the former Office of Planning and Institutional Assessment (OPIA) as well as the new Office for Learning Assessment, established to provide improved university-wide support for this key aspect of its educational mission. Formerly, Lance was the associate vice provost for institutional research at the University of Illinois, the executive director of the Center for the Study of Student Life at Ohio State, an associate director of institutional planning and research at the University of Florida, and a research associate in institutional research and planning at DePaul University. He attained his Bachelor of Arts in Sociology from Eastern Illinois University and his Master of Education and Doctorate in Higher Education Administration from the University of Nebraska.

Ross Markle, Ph.D., is the Senior Assessment Strategist in the Higher Education Division at Educational Testing Service (ETS). In his current role, he supports ETS' thought leadership efforts in higher education by collaborating with operational and research areas, as well as the higher education community. Ross also works directly with colleges and universities to promote the effective use of assessments and data in student success efforts, particularly with traditionally underserved populations. He has also worked in ETS' Research and Development Division, focusing on the assessment of noncognitive and twenty-first century skills, student success, and student learning outcomes assessment in higher education. Markle's current work focuses on assessing noncognitive skills to improve student success, training faculty and staff in effective student learning outcomes assessment processes, and measuring institutional outcomes such as civic competency and engagement and intercultural competence and diversity. Ross attained a Ph.D. in Assessment and Measurement Psychology from James Madison University, a master's degree in Industrial/Organizational Psychology from Middle Tennessee State University, and Bachelor's degree in Psychology from Edinboro University of Pennsylvania.

Jennifer Massey, Ph.D., is the Associate Vice President (Student Experience) at Western University in Ontario, Canada. Jennifer has more than 15 years of experience working in student affairs in Canada, the U.S., and the U.K. Among her professional colleagues in the field of student affairs, she is best known for her work in vision-casting, strategic planning, and assessment, which is distinguished by her steadfast commitment to student-centered learning and to sophisticated academic and administrative partnerships. Her work in this area has been recognized by professional organizations in both Canada and the United States, including the Canadian Association for College and University Student Services, the Canadian Association for Career and Educators and Employers, NASPA-Student Affairs Professionals in Higher Education, and ACPA-College Student Educators International. Her research interests include geographies of higher education, leadership and civic engagement, student development, cocurricular programming and academic achievement.

Kyle D. Massey, Ph.D., is the Coordinator for Evaluation, Data, and Project Management at Western University. Previously, he was a faculty member in the Faculty of Education at Memorial University of Newfoundland, where he taught undergraduate and graduate courses in the Postsecondary Studies program. He has previously held various administrative positions at several different colleges and universities in both the U.S. and Canada, including roles within student affairs and curricular management of academic programs. Kyle's research interests center on student affairs in the Canadian context, teaching and learning in higher education and faculty development.

Leah Ewing Ross, Ph.D., is Senior Director for Research and Initiatives with the Association for Institutional Research (AIR). She leads AIR's national research, scholarship, and innovation agenda to effectively position IR and related fields within the changing landscape of higher education. Leah collaborates with stakeholders to create forward-looking models to advance evidenced-based decision making, and to equip higher education professionals with the knowledge and tools they need as leaders within their organizations. Prior to AIR, she worked in consulting, scholarly publications, association management, and college admissions. Leah holds a Ph.D. in Educational Leadership from Iowa State University, M.S. in Higher Education Administration from Florida State University, and A.B. in English from Mount Holyoke College.

Javarro Russell, Ph.D., is a Senior Assessment Strategist in the Global Education Division at Educational Testing Service. Javarro obtained his doctorate in Assessment and Measurement from James Madison University. He has a background in consulting on measurement and assessment design issues in higher education. In his current role, he assists institutions in identifying solutions to assessing and measuring student learning outcomes on their campuses. He focuses on responding to critical questions about student learning for programs in general education and academic affairs, as well as student life. Javarro also specializes in identifying effective ways of reporting assessment results to audiences with varying levels of expertise in assessment and measurement. He is also the current President of the Northeastern Educational Research Association.

Jennifer Wells, Ph.D., is the Director of Assessment in the Office of Institutional Effectiveness, and an Assistant Professor of Higher Education in First-Year and Transition Studies, both at Kennesaw State University. Dr. Wells is the Editor for the Council for the Advancement of Standards in Higher Education (CAS), and she is facilitating the upcoming release of the 10th edition CAS book and Self-Assessment Guides (SAGs). Dr. Wells was previously the Director of Planning and Assessment in Student Affairs at Kennesaw State University. Jen earned her Ph.D. in College Student Affairs Administration from the University of Georgia; a Master's in Student Affairs Administration from Michigan State, and undergraduate degrees in German and History from Albion College. She served on the faculty for the ACPA Assessment Institute from 2012–2016 and has presented numerous times on various assessment topics including data hoarding, program review, qualitative data analysis, focus groups and interviews, and continuous improvement. Her research interests include psychosocial development and the broader autism phenotype, video games and social interactions, assessment, and continuous improvement.

Kimberly Yousey-Elsener, Ph.D., is the Director of Student Affairs Assessment and Strategic Initiatives at Binghamton University. Her experience in higher education includes coordinating student affairs and academic affairs assessment, teaching at the undergraduate and graduate level, residence life, academic advising/support, service learning, and student activities. She received her Ph.D. in Higher Education Administration and Policy from New York University. Her research interests include cultures of assessment and inquiry, capacity building in assessment, accreditation, and retention. Her publications focus on student affairs assessment.

About the Graduate Student Reviewers

Terell Bennett is a graduate student in Higher Education Counseling and Student Affairs at West Chester University. Terell's current graduate assistantship and internship experience is in West Chester University Residence Life and Housing Services. His future goals are to work in Student Affairs as Vice President/President of Student Affairs or potentially higher executive leadership positions at an institution, which includes potentially being a president of an institution.

Christopher G. Stancil is a graduate student in the Higher Education Policy and Student Affairs Program at West Chester University. His current Assistantship is in the Achieve! Program and Early Alert Program. His short-term goal is to conduct research within the Dean's office (CAH), present it, and possibly get research published, and his long-term goal is to be a Dean.

Lori Nicole Winters is a graduate student in the Higher Education Policy and Student Affairs Program at West Chester University. Her current assistantship/internship is as an Assessment and Planning Graduate Assistant; and Office of Sustainability Intern. Her future goal upon graduation is to find an opportunity within sustainability program management.

ACKNOWLEDGMENTS

This book would not have been possible without the contribution of so many thoughtful writers and reviewers. We assembled, what we believe, is the A-team of AER, and we are so thankful for their contributions. This talented group of authors includes:

S. Jeanne Horst, Ph.D.
Sara J. Finney, Ph.D.
Kimberly Yousey-Elsener, Ph.D.
Lance Kennedy-Phillips, Ph.D.
Leah Ewing Ross, Ph.D.
Jennifer Wells, Ph.D.
Martha Glass, Ph.D.
Ross Markle, Ph.D.
Javarro Russell, Ph.D.
R. Lorraine Bernotsky, D.Phil.
Jennifer Massey, Ph.D.
Kyle D. Massey, Ph.D.
Lisa J. Hatfield, Ed.D.

We especially want to thank three amazing graduate students who so graciously agreed to review several chapters of this book. Thank you **Terell Bennett, Lori Nicole Winters,** and **Christopher G. Stancil,** all from the Higher Education Policy and Student Affairs Program at West Chester University. Your insights/feedback mean so much to us. This book is written for you.

We offer a special thanks to Dennis Kouba for his excellent editorial skills and valuable feedback. You helped us bring this book to completion.

I have heard it said that the joy is in the journey, and I believe this now more than ever. Zeb, my dear friend and coeditor, thank you for going with me on this trip. To my dear loved ones who support me, even when I get a little too serious and tunneled vision. I share much love for and gratitude to Don,

Linda, Kim, Joyce, and my former OAI and PSU colleagues.—Vicki

I thank the creator of all things for the gifts that have been provided to all as we embarked upon this incredible journey. I want to also thank my wife and children for their support while I borrowed time from the family to complete this project. Last but not least, thank you Vic, my dear friend, respected colleague, and coeditor. You are amazing and as you know, this wouldn't have been possible without you.—Zeb

To all that read this book, read it with due diligence and purpose. You are the future of our discipline and this book is a tool that will aid in your success. To borrow from Sir Francis Bacon's famous quote, "Knowledge itself is power," we urge you to use the knowledge and wisdom shared in this book to open doors, create opportunities, and chart your paths for success.

CONTENTS

STUDENT AFFAIRS ASSESSMENT, EVALUATION, AND RESEARCH

Chapter 1

THE STATUS OF ASSESSMENT, EVALUATION, AND RESEARCH IN STUDENT AFFAIRS

Sara J. Finney & S. Jeanne Horst

The importance of and attention to assessment, evaluation, and research (AER) in higher education is not a recent phenomenon. Contemporary discussions and guidance regarding AER are firmly rooted in the contributions and insights of professionals who long preceded us. To frame the importance of AER in student affairs, we begin this chapter with a brief history of higher education outcomes assessment, with an emphasis on milestones within the domain of student affairs. As we will see, AER is ever-present throughout our history. We then highlight seminal AER documents and resources used to define, develop, and assess AER competencies. These seminal documents include the current *Professional Competency Areas for Student Affairs Educators* (American College Personnel Association & National Association of Student Personnel Administrators, 2015). Competency in AER is the focus of this book. We close the chapter with a discussion of the role of higher education and student affairs (HESA) graduate programs in building capacity in AER. As noted in the Preface, the goal of this book is to foster a student affairs practitioner's development of professional practice and identity based on the values, philosophy, and history of the profession. Thus, presenting this background information sets the stage for addressing and applying AER competency.

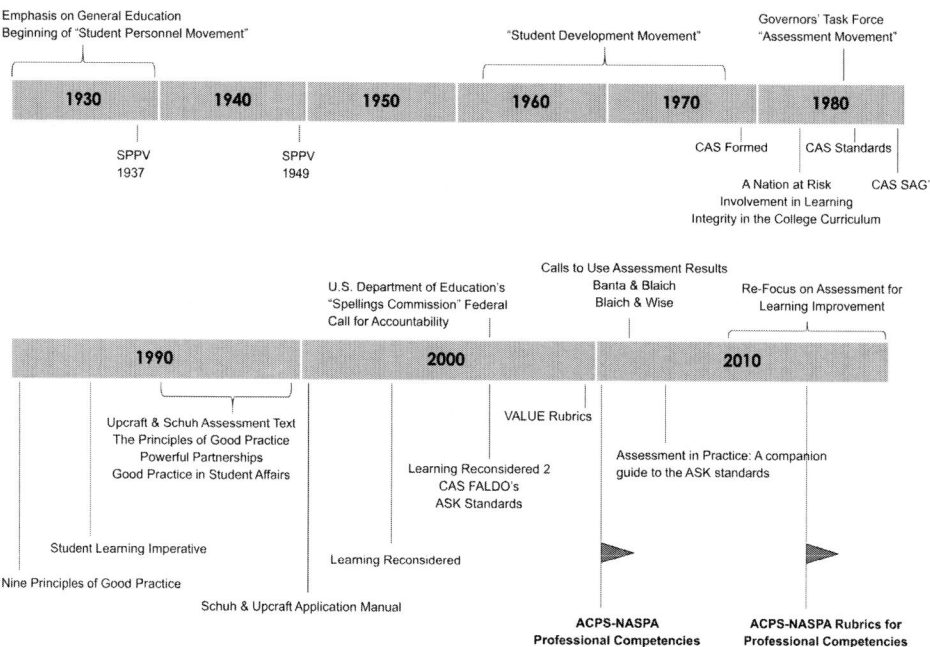

Figure 1.1. Timeline of major events with movements/calls to action on top of the timeline and documents on the bottom of timeline.

A Brief History of Outcomes Assessment in Higher Education

Although some may view student affairs assessment as a relatively new endeavor, it has deep roots in higher education, in fact, as early as the 1930s (see Figure 1.1). Moreover, it is impossible to disentangle the emergence of student affairs assessment from societal, governmental, and economic forces, as described below.

1930s to 1950s: The Underpinnings of Student Affairs Assessment

The history of student affairs assessment is couched within the broader history of higher education. Derived from the European university model, the U.S. university in the nineteenth century was economically and socially important to the industrial growth of the country (Altbach, 1991). During the post-Civil War era, colleges and universities focused primarily on students' intellect and acquisition of discipline-specific knowledge (American Council on Education, 1937). In the 1930s, there was a period of post-World War I growth in higher education that was accompanied by a shift from discipline-specific intellectualism to an emphasis on general education (Ewell, 1991). Early attempts at general education assessment were undertaken in the 1930s, such as the standardized testing for sophomores to seniors in the Pennsylvania Study and standardized testing in the Cooperative Study of General Education (Steedle, 2010).

Concurrent with the emphasis on general education (Ewell, 1991), the origin of student affairs assessment is traced to the 1937 American Council on Education publication, *The Student Personnel Point of View (SPPV)*. The SPPV emphasized focusing on "the student as a whole" (American Council on Education, 1937, p. 1), which represented the post-Civil-War shift from solely focusing upon students' acquisition of knowledge. The SPPV provided recommendations about the provision and evaluation of services for the whole student, including services built to foster skills, attitudes, and knowledge that now we consider important, such as civic engagement, sense of belonging, and ethical reasoning. The SPPV statement that student personnel programs should include an emphasis "on studies designed to evaluate and improve these functions and services" (American Council on Education, 1937, p. 4) foreshadowed the current emphasis on AER. The 1949 edition of the SPPV upheld the call for "A continuing program of evaluation of student personnel services and of the educational program to ensure the achievement by students of the objectives for which this program is designed" (American Council on Education, 1949, p. 29). Recommendations for types of evaluation data were broad, including student and faculty satisfaction, use of services, quality of staff training, and relationships between student affairs professionals and with faculty. Moreover, the importance of research from various domains (e.g., psychology, education, sociology) when developing and evaluating services is a major emphasis of the SPPV, which includes calls for continual evidence-based improvement that are still made today.

1960 to late 1970s: Focus on Program Evaluation and Student Development

Although called for in the early student affairs documents (American Council on Education, 1937, 1949), program evaluation in student affairs did not flourish until the 1960s and 1970s, running parallel with a broader societal trend toward large-scale government-funded programs (Ewell, 2002). Program evaluation involved systematic investigation of program effectiveness, typically in the form of program reviews and strategic plans; it led to a proliferation of surveys about student perceptions of and satisfaction with programs.

As well during this era, researchers examined student dispositions and behaviors, including ways in which student characteristics related to academic success (Kuh, Gonyea, & Rodriguez, 2002). Studies often focused on measuring aspects of student retention, attitudes, and cognitive gain, resulting in a proliferation of theories about student learning (Ewell, 2002). The trend influenced the creation of tools for assessing student characteristics. For example, the creation of a measure of student self-esteem (Rosenberg & Simmons, 1971) led to a proliferation of research about societal factors related to racial differences in student success.

The hallmark of this era was the student development movement: applying human development theories to college students. In the early 1970s, several seminal documents focused on student development and were targeted toward the student affairs professional. For example, the ACPA monograph *Student Development in Tomorrow's Higher Education: A Return to the Academy* (Brown, 1972) provided a critical review of student development and the role of student affairs personnel in promoting development. One recommendation was that "Colleges and universities should establish expectations for students and assess outcomes that cover the broad ranges of human behavior including the intellectual, personal-social, esthetic, cultural, and even the psychomotor dimensions" (Brown, 1972, p. 44). In short, the student development movement led to intentional student affairs programming, or "interventions" (Bloland, 1991, p. 3), aligned with and intended to promote student development.

Late 1970s to mid-1980s: Development and Distribution of the CAS Standards

Given the focus in the 1960s and 1970s on program evaluation, the formation of the Council for the Advancement of Standards in Higher Education (CAS) in 1979 was a natural next step. The result, in 1986, was a set of standards intended for quality assurance via program review and self-study of 16 functional areas (e.g., academic advising, career services, service-learning) and graduate professional preparation programs. In 1988, CAS provided Self-Assessment Guides (SAGs) as tools to identify program strengths and deficiencies, to enhance program impact on student learning and development, and to guide staff development.

The CAS standards, now in their ninth edition (Council for the Advancement of Standards in Higher Education, 2015), encompass 44 different functional areas, as well as a set of masters-level HESA academic program standards (http://www.cas.edu/standards). The CAS standards remain the most comprehensive collection of standards available for student affairs; they include standards of excellence, common ethical principles, and current student learning and development outcomes. Today, CAS consists of 41 higher education professional associations.

Underlying the CAS standards are a set of guiding principles or core beliefs, organized into five broad categories: students and their environment; diversity/multiculturalism; health engendering environments; organization, leadership, and human resources; and ethical considerations (Sharp, 2017). The early SPPV (1937) admonition to consider the student as a whole person remains evident within the CAS guiding principles. Undergirding each set of functional area standards are the General Standards (e.g., Mission, Program, Ethics, Assessment; Sharp, 2017), which provide a core framework for all areas and promote similarities across departments and institutions (Sharp, 2017). Note that assessment is a General Standard. In sum, the CAS standards set the stage for and remain prominent in the current-day emphasis on assessment of all student affairs programs.

Mid-1980s to 1990: Focus on Student Learning Rather than General Program Effectiveness

During the mid-1980s to 1990 era of educational reform, higher education leaders called for a focus on student learning. *A Nation at Risk* (Gardner, 1983) bemoaned the state of the educational system and called for major educational reforms. A year later, the National Institute of Education's Study Group on the Conditions of Excellence in American Higher Education published *Involvement in Learning* (1984). The study group included and was greatly influenced by education leader, Alexander Astin. The report authors emphasized that excellence in education must be centered on student learning, and that colleges should systematically assess their students' learning. Echoing a similar theme, the Association for American Colleges' report, *Integrity in the College Curriculum: A Report to the Academic Community* (1985), identified nine areas important to a liberal education curriculum (e.g., critical thinking, multicultural experiences) and included multiple calls for accountability and assessment.

Calls for accountability were further stimulated by a push from U.S. state governors. Governors' task forces were formed to address student learning concerns; their emphasis was on student learning outcomes assessment data (Ashcroft, 1986). The task forces recommended that "States should insist that colleges assess what students actually learn while in college" (Alexander, 1986, p. 202). The task forces also encouraged accrediting bodies to hold colleges and universities accountable for providing evidence of student learning. The work of the task forces culminated in two influential National Governors' Association reports encouraging U.S. educational reform. One report questioned the extent to which students learn during college (Alexander, Clinton, & Kean, 1986). The other report noted a lack of consensus about the definition of "assessment" and recommended allocation of resources for improving assessment programs (Education Commission of the States, 1986). The reports led to the "assessment movement" (Ewell, 2002, p. 7), which called for governors to require institutions to assess student learning in order to document the magnitude of learning and to evaluate program quality.

1990s to 2000: Commitment to Learning Outcomes Assessment "On Paper," not "Practice"

The multiple reports generated during the previous decade led to a commitment to learning outcomes assessment "on paper." However, although assessment was mandated in most U.S. states by the 1990s, there was no consistency in definition or practice (Ewell, 2002). The lack of congruence between what was called for "on paper" and what was done in practice led to the creation of several important documents further rationalizing the need for and clarifying the characteristics of student learning outcomes assessment.

First, the American Association for Higher Education (AAHE, 1992) created the *Nine Principles of Good Practice for Assessing Student Learning,* which provided clear criteria for incorporating assessment of student learning into higher education. Then, an ACPA (1994) publication, *The Student Learning Imperative: Implications for Student Affairs,* called for the intentional creation of programming that fosters student learning, where student learning is considered cognitive competence and interpersonal competence. The report clearly emphasized the necessity for student affairs professionals to be experts in student learning and development. It further noted the importance of assessment data in the creation of programs.

A few years later, in 1997, ACPA and NASPA published *The Principles of Good Practice for Student Affairs* to provide a short summary of what practices were most likely to support student learning as suggested by research (e.g., good practice engages students in active learning; good practice uses systematic inquiry to improve student performance). Each of the seven principles has an associated inventory of items designed to determine the level of consistency of the programming with the principle of good practice. Importantly, it furthered the call for high-quality learning outcomes data by stating that student affairs professionals are educators who should ask, "What are students learning from our programs and services and how can their learning be enhanced?" (ACPA & NASPA, 1997, para.15). Answering this question involves collecting, interpreting, and then using learning outcomes data: "Student affairs educators who are skilled in using assessment methods acquire high-quality information; effective application of this information to practice results in programs and change strategies that improve institutional and student achievement" (ACPA & NASPA, 1997, para. 15).

Good Practice in Student Affairs: Principles to Foster Student Learning (Blimling & Whitt, 1999) was a follow-up and practical guide for implementing *The Principles of Good Practice for Student Affairs*. Additionally, AAHE, ACPA, and NASPA published *Powerful Partnerships: A Shared Responsibility for Student Learning* (1998), which stressed that assessment was an essential mechanism to improve student learning.

2000 to 2006: Influx of Materials to Guide Assessment Practice in Student Affairs

The student affairs community created materials to spur actual practice of assessment to answer the continued, compelling calls for learning outcomes assessment. *Assessment in Student Affairs: A Guide for Practitioners* (Upcraft & Schuh, 1996) and its companion guide *Assessment Practice in Student Affairs: An Applications Manual* (Schuh, Upcraft, & Associates, 2001) are likely the most well-known textbooks to support student affairs assessment practice broadly. The texts provide a mechanism for skill development and informed engagement in assessment.

NASPA and ACPA published *Learning Reconsidered: A Campus-Wide Focus on the Student Experience* (Keeling, 2004) and a practice-focused companion document, *Learning Reconsidered 2: Implementing a Campus-Wide Focus on the Student Experience* (Keeling, 2006). These influential documents broadened the conceptualizations of learning beyond the classroom, emphasizing that student affairs personnel should work with academic affairs personnel to provide learning experiences and to assess the learning associated with those experiences. *Learning Reconsidered 2* provides tools and templates for designing outcomes assessment, undergirded by the necessity of learning theory for effective assessment; it is useful to those conducting student affairs assessment.

The renewed focus on student learning outcomes assessment was also evident in the updated 2003 CAS standards, which included 16 student learning and development domains (Council for the Advancement of Standards in Higher Education, 2015). In 2006, CAS published *The Frameworks for Assessing Learning and Development Outcomes (FALDOs)*, which served as a practice-focused companion to the 2003 student learning outcomes. The FALDOs provide a resource that enables practitioners to conduct assessment focused on learning and development, rather than simply reporting satisfaction with program services.

The FALDOs remain a significant resource and exemplar for student learning outcomes assessment despite the fact that the specific learning domains quickly became outdated in 2008 when the CAS standards were revised in response to *Learning Reconsidered 2*. In the 2008 CAS revision, the original 16 student learning and development domains were reframed as six domains (knowledge acquisition, construction integration, and application; cognitive complexity; intrapersonal development; interpersonal competence; humanitarianism and civic engagement; and practical competence). To date, assessment is prominent in the CAS standards, which specify that all programs need to assess student learning and development, use assessment results, and share assessment results with stakeholders.

2006 to 2010: National Calls for and Efforts Toward Learning Outcomes Assessment

Even with the increased emphasis on assessment and the creation of materials to support the practice of assessment, at this point there was little consistent action. "Despite many calls for outcomes assessment and data?based decision making in student affairs, there have been only a few examples illustrating efforts in the field to respond wholeheartedly or effectively to these calls" (Taskforce on the Future of Student Affairs, 2010, p. 3). Noting the deficiency, Secretary of Education Margaret Spellings, revitalized and further solidified the importance of student learning assessment. In what has become known as the "Spellings Commission," *A Test of Leadership: Charting the Future of U.S. Higher Education* (U.S. Department of Education, 2006) held institutions of higher education accountable for student learning.

The Association of American Colleges and Universities (AAC&U) took the charge seriously, implementing several initiatives. One initiative, the Valid Assessment of Learning in Undergraduate Education (VALUE) rubrics (Rhodes, 2009), provided frameworks for student learning outcomes in a variety of domains crucial to a liberal education. These domains included teamwork, civic engagement, and problem solving. First released in 2009, the VALUE rubrics were an initiative to develop direct assessments of student learning (available at www.aacu.org/VALUE/rubrics). Another AAC&U (2011) initiative, Liberal Education and America's Promise (LEAP), outlined a set of Essential Learning Outcomes: knowledge of human cultures and the physical and natural world; intellectual and practical skills (e.g., critical thinking and communication); personal and social responsibility (e.g., civic engagement, intercultural competence, and ethical reasoning); and integrative and applied learning. Also identified were "high impact practices" (AAC&U, 2011, p. 15) believed to support student achievement of the Essential Learning Outcomes, of which at least five are clearly related to student affairs practice: first-year experiences, study abroad, service learning in courses, diversity experiences, and learning communities. In short, AAC&U's LEAP initiative lent further credence to the importance of assessing learning associated with student affairs programs, while providing resources (i.e., VALUE rubrics) to do so.

Of particular importance to student affairs during this time period was the development of AER standards and competencies for student affairs professionals (ACPA, 2006; ACPA & NASPA, 2010). As discussed below, the *Assessment Skills and Knowledge (ASK) Standards* (ACPA, 2006) were the first set of standards developed to articulate the knowledge, skills, and dispositions necessary for student affairs professionals to measure student learning and development outcomes. The ACPA/ NASPA AER competencies, the focus of this book, were developed a few years later and expanded upon the ASK Standards.

2010 to Today: Renewed Focus on Learning Improvement

It is safe to say that, by 2010, most institutions had some type of assessment process in place, with many making efforts primarily due to accountability mandates. There was a clearly-identified "tension" (Ewell, 2009, p. 7) between assessment efforts conducted for accountability purposes versus assessment efforts focused on providing evidence of learning improvement. Although many institutions were busy assessing student learning, there was little evidence that assessment data were actually used to improve student learning (Banta & Blaich, 2011; Blaich & Wise, 2011; Kuh et al., 2015).

Efforts are underway to clearly articulate what is meant by "learning improvement." One prominent definition provides the following model: (1) assessment of student learning, (2) use of assessment data to inform changes to programming, (3) reassessment that provides evidence of improved student learning (Fulcher, Good, Coleman, & Smith, 2014; Fulcher, Smith, Sanchez, Ames, & Meixner, 2017). At the core of this model is the idea that it is not enough to repeatedly assess student learning; we must use data to make evidence-based changes to the program to foster greater learning. This idea of continual improvement is not new. It was present in the SPPV and discussions in the 1980s, but for many institutions it has been trumped by assessment for accountability purposes (Ewell, 2009).

AER Standards: Resources to Articulate, Build, and Assess Competencies

As mentioned during the review of the history of outcomes assessment, one hallmark of the profession of student affairs involved the creation of several seminal documents specifically focused on assessment skills necessary for professionals. Below we spotlight two documents outlining the currently endorsed competencies in AER. We then note contemporary resources that support building and evaluating such competencies.

Articulating Professional Standards and Competencies: Seminal Documents

ACPA's Commission for Assessment for Student Development, which formed in 2004 and was renamed in 2006 to ACPA's Commission for Assessment and Evaluation, created the *Assessment Skills and Knowledge (ASK) Standards* (ACPA, 2006). Prior to this document, there was no organized articulation of the specific skills student affairs professionals need to effectively assess student-learning outcomes. The ASK standards detailed what *all* student affairs professionals should know and be able to do related to outcomes assessment regardless of functional area. The standards are divided into 13 areas: assessment design; articulating learning and development outcomes; selection of data collection and management methods; assessment instruments; surveys used for assessment purposes; interviews and focus groups used for assessment purposes; analysis; benchmarking; program review and evaluation; assessment ethics; effective reporting and use of results; politics of assessment; and assessment education. Each content area includes two to nine statements describing the competencies that student affairs professionals should possess to meet the content standard. Importantly, the ASK Standards have been endorsed by accrediting bodies (e.g., Western Association of Schools and Colleges), and by AAC&U (Henning, Mitchell, & Maki, 2008).

Several years later, ACPA and NASPA collaborated (in the Joint Task Force on Professional Competencies and Standards) to create a common set of *Professional Competency Areas* for student affairs educators (ACPA & NASPA, 2010). As detailed in Chapter 2, these competencies were revised in 2015 and consist of 10 areas, of which Assessment, Evaluation, and Research (AER) is one. Distinctions between the AER terms, along with the intersection between the competency areas, are discussed in Chapter 2. In brief, each of the 10 competency areas specify knowledge, skills, and dispositions expected of *all* professionals, regardless of functional area or specialization within the field. These competencies can be used for position descriptions, professional development experiences, graduate preparation programs, content for conferences, and communicating student affairs professional work to others, among other uses. With respect to AER, professionals must have "the ability to use, design, conduct, and critique qualitative and quantitative AER analyses; to manage organizations using AER processes and the results obtained from them; and to shape the political and ethical climate surrounding AER processes and uses on campus" (ACPA & NASPA, 2015; p. 8)

The *Professional Competency Areas* elaborate on the *ASK Standards* by describing the assessment skills of competent professionals and categorizing the level of these skills as "foundational," "intermediate," or "advanced." Otherwise, the basic content of the two documents is quite similar.

In contrast to the *ASK Standards* and the *Professional Competency Areas,* which articulate professionals' assessment competencies, the *CAS Standards* aid in creating and evaluating programs that contribute to student learning (Council for the Advancement of Standards in Higher Education, 2015). The *CAS Standards* articulate the desired qualities of the program (e.g., program has student learning and development outcomes, program changes are informed by assessment results, program is associated with evidence-based improvements, program is associated with ongoing cycle of assessment, program has adequate resources to engage in assessment). With the program as the focus, the CAS standards can be used to inform and guide improvement to programming, which can then serve as a powerful advertising mechanism if programs meet these standards. Thus, the *CAS Standards* serve a different purpose than the *ASK Standards* and the *Professional Competency Areas.* With that said, it is professionals with the competencies articulated in these two latter documents who can create programming that meets assessment-related CAS standards.

As a result of student affairs assessment being situated within a broader context, there are additional standards to which we must adhere. Specifically, assessment is typically situated within, or highly connected to, university offices of institutional research, which maintain their own professional code of ethics (Association for Institutional Research, 2013). Moreover, whenever professionals create and administer tests, they are bound by standards for educational and psychological testing (AERA, APA, NCME, 2014). Finally, given that the end goal of assessment endeavors is to evaluate program impact on student learning and development, the *Program Evaluation Standards* (Yarbrough, Shula, Hopson, & Caruthers, 2010) are invaluable.

Building and Evaluating Professional's Personal Competencies: Current Resources

Development of AER knowledge and skills requires more than the clear articulation of those competencies; it requires intentional activities and materials to support skill development in addition to feedback regarding personal competency. The following resources, some of which are the focus of this book, offer support for those who teach or wish to learn and then evaluate current AER competencies.

With respect to teaching and learning, the *Assessment Education Framework,* created in 2005 by NASPA's Assessment, Evaluation, and Research Knowledge Community, is a three-page document that simply outlines the topics necessary for building assessment competency for both new and continuing professionals (e.g., "Assessment 100: Beginning Concepts and Overview of the Process; Assessment 110: Articulating Purpose and Mapping Activities). The actual content of each program is not available. Instead, the outlines are used to create or select training sessions at annual conferences, such as the NASPA or ACPA, or at assessment conferences such as the NASPA Assessment and Persistence Conferences or the ACPA Student Affairs Assessment Institute.

Assessment in Practice: A Companion Guide to the ASK Standards (Timm, Barham, McKinney, & Knerr, 2013) provides both an introduction to assessment-related concepts and case studies that illustrate the assessment process at different types of institutions. The explicit focus in each chapter on one ASK Standard enables novices to familiarize themselves with the various aspects of assessment without being overwhelmed. This approach also enables continuing professionals to direct their attention to specific concepts or examples that need refreshing.

Just as *Assessment in Practice: A Companion Guide to the ASK Standards* provides resources for meeting the specific ASK Standards, the chapters you will read in this book are purposefully aligned for building the ACPA/NASPA AER competencies. Similarly, *Student Affairs Assessment: Theory to Practice* (Henning & Roberts, 2016) provides a didactic treatment of essential assessment concepts and skills, mapping the AER competency areas to each chapter of their book, with the chapters targeting the foundational level of the competency area.

Going beyond documents, on-line professional development in student affairs assessment is facilitated by NASPA's Assessment, Evaluation, and Research Knowledge Community and Student Affairs Assessment Leaders (SAAL). Both organizations offer incredible capacity building supports through their websites or listservs.

With respect to evaluating skill sets and providing actionable feedback, the rubrics for assessing mastery of the AER competencies are extremely valuable (ACPA & NASPA, 2016), given that the AER competencies and the ASK standards don't easily allow for self-assessment. As discussed in Chapter 2, the rubrics are intentionally aligned with professional competency areas (ACPA & NASPA, 2015). This alignment enables professionals to assess the knowledge, skills, and dispositions for self-assessment, student feedback during graduate program completion, or staff feedback during annual performance reviews. Given the detailed nature of the rubric and the ability to identify the level of one's skills as foundational, intermediate, or advanced, the resulting information can be used to identify areas of growth to target with professional development.

Growth of HESA Graduate Programs and Intentional Training in AER

Given the competencies expected of student affairs professionals, we now turn our attention to formal training programs that can support such skill development. We begin our discussion by reviewing the emergence of student services, which ultimately necessitated formal training programs. That is, understanding the need for professionals to create, offer, and assess student services informs the type of training necessary to engage competently in the profession.

Need for Student Services Led to Formal Training of Student Affairs Professionals

Changes in the landscape of higher education—increasing enrollment, increasing diversity, and increasing numbers of students who face challenges—led to a growing need for student services on campus. It is now commonplace for colleges to provide personal support services, such as counseling and disability services, as well as programming intended to meet increasing demands for workplace skills, such as multicultural competency (Hamrick & Klein, 2015). Not only are student affairs professionals central to meeting the variety of student needs, but they are asked to show evidence of the quality of this work (Hamrick & Klein, 2015; Tull & Kuk, 2012).

The need for and proliferation of these student services was accompanied by an increase in higher education and student affairs (HESA) graduate programs. HESA graduate programs have become one of the main routes for entering the field of student affairs (Tull & Kuk, 2012). Estimates of the exact number of HESA programs differ depending upon the source from which program information is obtained. Based upon the ACPA directory, there were approximately 157 HESA programs in 2014, which may be an underestimate, given that some programs may not be included because of ACPA fees and the requirement that programs submit a CAS self-study (Ortiz, Filimon, & Cole-Jackson, 2015). Based upon the NASPA directory, there were approximately 142 HESA-like programs in 2014. Regardless of source from which HESA estimates are obtained, the number of HESA programs almost doubled between 1999 and 2014 (Ortiz et al., 2015).

Importance of Training HESA Graduate Students in Learning Theory

As noted above, in the late twentieth century, there was a call to make an impact on student learning via student services. *Learning Reconsidered* (Keeling, 2004) clarified that learning is not considered simply the acquisition of information, but is viewed as transformative and includes aspects of student development (e.g., humanitarianism). The student affairs professional is now perceived as an educator, providing potentially high-impact curricular programming. Thus, student affairs professionals have a responsibility to be familiar with research that is relevant to their students' learning and development (Hatfield & Wise, 2015), and must understand the basic forms of learning, such as experiential learning, integration and transfer of knowledge, and other foundational concepts related to learning (Barber, 2006). Put simply, to build programs to impact learning, professionals must be knowledgeable about student learning theory.

Training in learning theory is not only critical for building high-impact programming, it is also imperative to effectively assess the impact of programming on student learning and development (Bresciani, 2010). This intersection between competencies in AER and competencies in student learning and development is discussed in Chapter 2. HESA graduate programs have a tremendous opportunity to prepare professionals to be knowledgeable about student learning, how to build programs to impact learning, and how to assess the impact on learning.

Importance of Training HESA Graduate Students in AER

Both faculty and employers have said they value AER competencies, as indicated in four empirical studies. A 2010 study explored HESA faculty perceptions of the importance of *intended* learning outcomes of graduate preparation programs (Herdlein, Kline, Boquard, & Haddad, 2010). Assessment skills were rated "very important." When asked to prioritize the importance of curricular topics, the majority of faculty placed development and learning theories as the highest priority, with assessment and research nearing the top.

Systematic mixed-methods studies of job postings showed that employers also value proficiency in AER (Hoffman & Bresciani, 2010; 2012). More specifically, AER competencies were listed as desired skills for applicants, particularly when positions required graduate training.

A 2013 meta-analysis of valued competencies for student affairs professionals as indicated by graduate faculty, graduate students, senior student affairs officers (SSAOs), and new professionals identified AER as the most frequently desired skill (Herdlein, Riefler, & Mrowka, 2013). Notably, this desire for AER proficiency increased compared to earlier meta-analytic studies that summarized necessary skills of competent student affairs professionals.

Collectively, these recent empirical studies indicate that it is critical to educate HESA students in the domain of AER. Likewise, when discussing the implications of the current educational environment on the ability of the student affairs field to survive and thrive, the Task Force on the Future of Student Affairs (2010) emphasized the need for competency in AER: "All student affairs practitioners, regardless of functional area, must approach their work with the assumption that all aspects of it must be supported by evidence gathered through accepted modes of assessment and consistent with the research about college student success" (p. 10). Importantly, this demand for AER competency is not new; it echoes the repeated decades-old calls for theory-based program development and assessment (e.g., American Council on Education, 1937, 1949).

Thus, we encourage graduate students to not only hear those calls, but to react. Be proactive with respect to building AER skills. Specifically, we recommend students evaluate their AER skills at multiple points during their HESA program journey to identify if professional development is necessary. Moreover, the simple act of evaluating AER skills increases familiarity with AER vocabulary, showcases the inter-connectedness of AER skills, and highlights the level of competency expected in the AER domain in order to engage in effective practice. The same recommendations apply to new professionals in the field. We suggest the use of the AER rubrics for these purposes, as discussed in Chapter 2.

Chapter 2

DEVELOPMENT OF COMPETENCIES IN ASSESSMENT, EVALUATION, AND RESEARCH, WITH TERMS AND CONCEPTS

KIMBERLY YOUSEY-ELSENER

Professional competencies guide student affairs' professionals in their growth and development as these competencies identify specific skills and attributes needed to be successful in the field. Building from Chapter 1, this chapter focuses more deeply on the development of the competencies and how to use them. This chapter also lays the foundation for future chapters focused solely on assessment, evaluation, and research.

History of the Competencies

In 2009–2010 the American College Personnel Association (ACPA), through its College Student Educators International, and the National Association of Student Personnel Administrators (NASPA), through its Student Affairs Administrators in Higher Education, created a Joint Task Force on Professional Competencies and Standards. This task force was "charged with drafting a document that articulated common professional competency areas applicable to all student affairs professionals in the United States, regardless of their specific area of emphasis within the field" (ACPA & NASPA, 2010, p. 3). The task force began its work in October 2009 by reviewing related literature, relevant NASPA and ACPA documents (such as the Student Learning Imperative, ASK Standards), and the Council for the Advancement of Standards in Higher Education (CAS) work on professional ethics and learning outcomes. Once the task force agreed on a final set of 10 competencies (ACPA & NASPA, 2010), small working teams determined the content under each competency area.

The result was a common set of Professional Competency Areas for student affairs educators. This common set was comprised of 10 competency areas, organized around three levels (basic, intermediate, and advanced) as well as three threads that were designated as essential components connected with all of the competencies: technology, sustainability, and globalism. The 10 competency areas were Advising and Helping; Assessment, Evaluation, and Research; Equity, Diversity, and Inclusion; Ethical Professional Practice; History, Philosophy, and Values; Human and Organizational Resources; Law, Policy, and Governance; Leadership; Personal Foundations; and Student Learning and Development.

The task force finished its work in summer 2010, issuing a final recommendation that the competencies be reviewed and updated regularly to allow for changes in the field moving forward. In summer 2011, as part of the evolution of the competencies, a second team of assessment professionals was convened to create a companion set of rubrics. The ACPA/NASPA Professional Competencies Rubrics (ACPA & NASPA, 2011) were designed to provide an assessment tool around each of the 10 competency areas for self-reflection, reflection with supervisors, or for use in graduate preparation programs.

In 2014, ACPA and NASPA joined forces once again to create the Professional Competencies Task Force. This task force was charged with "reviewing the professional competencies and recommending changes as needed" (ACPA & NASPA, 2016, 2015, p. 4). The task force reviewed the Professional Competency Areas developed in 2010, returned to the literature, considered recommendations made by ACPA's Digital Task Force and NASPA's Technology Knowledge Community, and solicited feedback from members who were currently using the 2010 competencies. While the Professional Competency Areas for Student Affairs Educators (ACPA & NASPA, 2015) consisted of 10 competencies, most of which were the same as the 2010 version, several changes occurred:

• Equity, Diversity, and Inclusion was altered to Social Justice and Inclusion, reflecting a more action-oriented focus of the field and a focus on an active process.

- Technology was originally a thread that was intended to be interwoven throughout all of the competencies, but review by the task force revealed that "an unintended consequence was that technology was often omitted from practical applications of the competencies" (p. 5). Therefore, Technology was designated as a distinct competency.
- Advising and Helping was changed to Advising and Supporting, with the goal of empowering college students through relationships, as compared to only directing students. It was also meant to distinguish competency in student affairs professions from those skills needed by health care professionals (e.g., counselors, psychologists, nurse practitioners) who provide a different kind of help on college campuses.
- Ethical Professional Practice was combined with Personal Foundations to create the Personal and Ethical Foundations competency.

The changes in 2015 resulted in the 10 competencies shown in Table 2.1. The remaining conversation in this book focuses on this latest version of the standards published in 2015.

As well, a set of rubrics was developed to assist in assessing skill levels associated with these competencies (ACPA/NASPA Professional Competencies Rubrics, 2016). More details about the rubrics are provided later in this chapter. The competencies were developed with multiple uses in mind. An obvious application is that professionals can utilize the competencies to assess their areas of strengths and areas needing improvement, in other words, setting goals for professional development. In addition, the competencies can serve as curriculum guides for graduate preparation programs and conference planners. While the competencies are not intended to be directly connected to specific functional areas, they can also be used when formulating job descriptions, position descriptions, and performance evaluations. And finally, the competencies are meant to serve as an advocacy tool to help promote the profession and outreach to those interested in the field.

Table 2.1
PROFESSIONAL COMPETENCY AREAS FOR
STUDENT AFFAIRS PRACTITIONERS, 2010 AND 2015

Professional Competency Areas for Student Affairs Practitioners, 2010	*Professional Competency Areas of Student Affairs Educators, 2015*
Advising and Helping	Advising and Supporting
Assessment, Evaluation, and Research	Assessment, Evaluation, and Research
Equity, Diversity, and Inclusion	Social Justice and Inclusion
Ethical Professional Practice	Personal and Ethical Foundations
Personal Foundations	
History, Philosophy, and Values	Values, Philosophy, and History
Human and Organizational Resources	Organizational and Human Resources
Law, Policy and Governance	Law, Policy, and Governance
Leadership	Leadership
Student Learning and Development	Student Learning and Development
	Technology

The Competencies

The Professional Competency Areas for Student Affairs Educators (2015) outlined 10 competencies that span the various functional areas of student affairs and encompass the key skills, knowledge, and dispositions essential in professional practice. Each of the competencies was first defined (Table 2.2); then, specific outcomes were created for each competency at the foundational, intermediate, and advanced levels.

Foundational, Intermediate, and Advanced Levels

The foundational, intermediate, and advanced levels under each competency serve two functions. First, they provide a gauge for professionals at different times during their careers. It would be expected

Table 2.2
COMPETENCY AREAS

Competency Area	Description
Personal and Ethical Foundations (PEF)	"Involves the knowledge, skills, and dispositions to develop and maintain integrity in one's life and work; this includes thoughtful development, critique, and adherence to a holistic and comprehensive standard of ethics and commitment to one's own wellness and growth. Personal and ethical foundations are aligned because integrity has an internal locus informed by a combination of external ethical guidelines, an internal voice of care, and our own lived experiences. Our personal and ethical foundations grow through a process of curiosity, refection, and self-authorship" (p. 12).
Values, Philosophy, and History (VPH)	"Involves knowledge, skills, and dispositions that connect the history, philosophy, and values of the student affairs profession to one's current professional practice. This competency area embodies the foundations of the profession from which current and future research, scholarship, and practice will change and grow. The commitment to demonstrating this competency area ensures that our present and future practices are informed by an understanding of the profession's history, philosophy, and values" (p. 12).
Assessment, Evaluation, and Research (AER)	"Focuses on the ability to design, conduct, critique, and use various AER methodologies and the results obtained from them, to utilize AER processes and their results to inform practice, and to shape the political and ethical climate surrounding AER processes and uses in higher education " (p. 12).
Law, Policy, and Governance (LPG)	"Includes the knowledge, skills, and dispositions relating to policy development processes used in various contexts, the application of legal constructs, compliance/policy issues, and the understanding of governance structures and their impact on one's professional practice" (p. 13).
Organizational and Human Resources (OHR)	"Includes knowledge, skills, and dispositions used in the management of institutional human capital, financial, and physical resources. This competency area recognizes that student affairs professionals bring personal strengths and grow as managers t hrough challenging themselves to build new skills in the selection, supervision, motivation, and formal evaluation of staff; resolution of conflict; management of the politics of organizational discourse; and the effective application of strategies and techniques associated with financial resources, facilities management, fundraising, technology, crisis management, risk management and sustainable resources" (p. 13).

Table 2.2—*Continued*

Competency Area	Description
Leadership (LEAD)	"Addresses the knowledge, skills, and dispositions required of a leader, with or without positional authority. Leadership involves both the individual role of a leader and the leadership process of individuals working together to envision, plan, and affect change in organizations and respond to broad-based constituencies and issues. This can include working with students, student affairs colleagues, faculty, and community members" (p. 13).
Social Justice and Inclusion (SJI)	"While there are many conceptions of social justice and inclusion in various contexts, for the purposes of this competency area, it is defined here as both a process and a goal which includes the knowledge, skills, and dispositions needed to create learning environments that foster equitable participation of all groups while seeking to address and acknowledge issues of oppression, privilege, and power. This competency involves student affairs educators who have a sense of their own agency and social responsibility that includes others, their community, and the larger global context. Student affairs educators may incorporate social justice and inclusion competencies into their practice through seeking to meet the needs of all groups, equitably distributing resources, raising social consciousness, and repairing past and current harms on campus communities" (p. 14).
Student Learning and Development (SLD)	"Addresses the concepts and principles of student development and learning theory. This includes the ability to apply theory to improve and inform student affairs and teaching practice" (p. 14).
Technology (TECH)	"Focuses on the use of digital tools, resources, and technologies for the advancement of student learning, development, and success as well as the improved performance of student affairs professionals. Included within this area are knowledge, skills, and dispositions that lead to the generation of digital literacy and digital citizenship within communities of students, student affairs professionals, faculty members, and colleges and universities as a whole" (p. 15).
Advising and Supporting (A/S)	"Addresses the knowledge, skills, and dispositions related to providing advising and support to individuals and groups through direction, feedback, critique, referral, and guidance. Through developing advising and supporting strategies that take into account self-knowledge and the needs of others, we play critical roles in advancing the holistic wellness of ourselves, our students, and our colleagues" (p. 15).

that newer professionals might find themselves at the more foundational or intermediate level while those who have been in the field
longer and have developed more as professionals may find themselves
at the intermediate or advanced levels. As noted in Chapter 1, professionals can determine their levels of proficiency by using the
Assessment Skills and Knowledge (ASK) Standards (ACPA, 2006) to self
assess their knowledge, skills, and dispositions related to outcomes
assessment regardless of functional area. It is important to note that
the levels are not linked with time in the profession, but can align with
professional interests or passions. For example, a newer professional
who has a passion for assessment and therefore may have done extensive research and work in that area during graduate school, may be at
the intermediate or advanced level in assessment, evaluation, and
research compared to a professional who has been working for several years but has never had direct assessment responsibilities. As noted
in the competencies, "Advancement in rank is not a guarantee of high-
er-order proficiency" (p. 8). Second, the levels are meant to show progression through a competency. The task force suggested, "mastering
the foundational skills in every competency area should be a professional development priority" (ACPA & NASPA, 2015, p. 8), but also
suggested that the outcomes should not be seen as a checklist. Just as
our students often develop socially and cognitively in a nonlinear fash-
ion, so too do professionals. One could reach the intermediate level
in some outcomes, but not all, and then need to go back to foundational elements in order to build a stronger base before developing
further.

Intersections of the Competencies

The 10 competencies were designed to stand alone as distinct sets
of skills, knowledge, and dispositions; however, there is also consider-
able overlap between each of the competencies. Just as student affairs
professionals do not function each day jumping from one skill set to
another (e.g., I'm going to advise from 9:00 a.m. to 10:00 a.m., lead
from 10:00 a.m. to 11:00 a.m., use technology from 11:00 a.m. to noon,
etc.) so too should the competencies be thought of as areas that intersect at different points in a person's development.

Though each outcome is aligned primarily with just one competency, well over half of the outcomes intersect with other areas. This sug-

gests that professional development work in any one competency area is related to work in multiple other areas (ACPA & NASPA, 2015, p. 9).

This overlap begins at the foundational level but grows to be more complex as one moves to the advanced level in each of the competencies. For example, in assessment, evaluation, and research, a foundational level outcome is "Design program and learning outcomes that are appropriately clear, specific, measurable. . ." (p. 20). This involves very little overlap with the other competencies except perhaps Student Learning and Development. But at the intermediate level, "Prioritize program and learning outcomes with organizational goals and values," that same skill set of designing and developing outcomes now intersects with competencies such as Leadership, Organizational and Human Resources, and possibly Law, Policy, and Governance. At the advanced level one might also employ Advising and Supporting as one moves from designing outcomes to teaching others how to design outcomes. A visual representation of this overlap helps to show the progression at various levels of development (Figure 2.1).

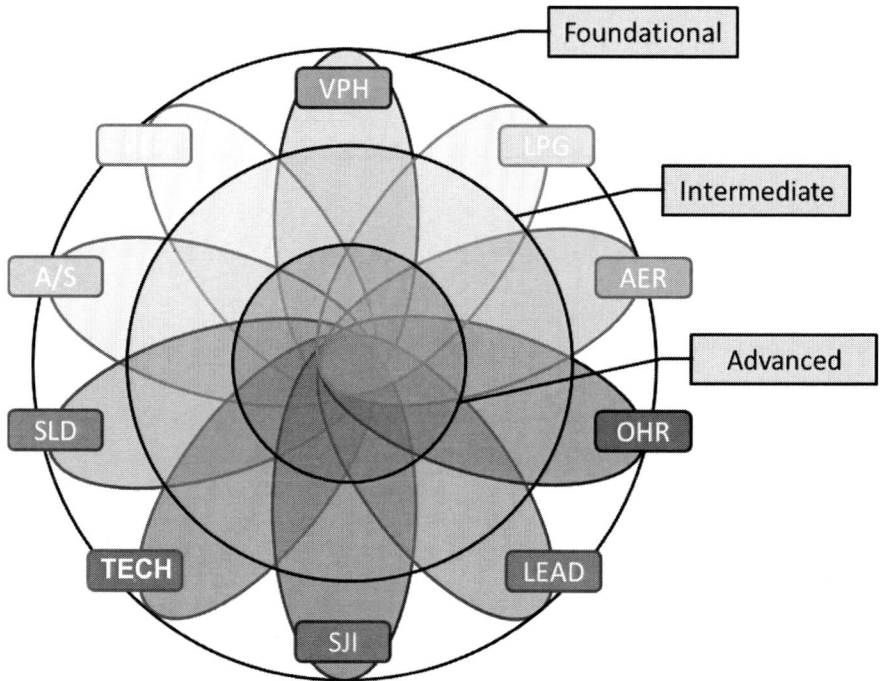

Figure 2.1. Visual Representation of the Intersection of the 10 Competency Areas. (With permission: Professional Competency Areas of Student Affairs Educators, 2015, p. 8.)

When planning professional development around the competencies, it is important to keep these intersections in mind, as development in one competency may be dependent upon development in another.

Assessment, Evaluation, and Research

As noted in Chapter 1, describing competencies in the areas of assessment, evaluation, and research has been a topic for many decades. As assessment becomes more prolific in higher education, these skills are now an essential part of a student affairs professional's portfolio. *Professional Competency Areas for Student Affairs Educators* (2015) groups Assessment, Evaluation, and Research (AER) into one competency.

The Assessment, Evaluation, and Research competency area focuses on one's ability to design, conduct, critique, and use various AER methodologies and the results obtained from them; to utilize AER processes and their results to inform practice; and to shape the political and ethical climate surrounding AER processes and uses in higher education (p. 20).

While the task force chose to group these three concepts together, it is important to recognize the similarities and differences between them in order to better understand the competencies themselves.

Assessment. The definitions of assessment are as varied as the purposes of conducting assessment; both term and practice have evolved over time. For example, assessment was defined as a process to collect data: "Any efforts to gather, analyze and interpret evidence which describes institutional, departmental, divisional or agency effectiveness" (Upcraft & Schuh, 1996, p. 18). More recently it has been defined as a process that involves setting goals, measuring progress, and using data to inform decisions. The greatest shift has been to an increased focus on the use of data in decision making.

In recent years, it has become clear that while most people understand the need for gathering data for the purposes of assessment, institutions and professionals are falling short in using that data to improve practice. Michael Middaugh suggests that "any . . . accreditor will say that the problem is no longer one of getting institutions to engage in assessment . . . rather, the difficulty is in getting institutions to close the loop and actually use the data for . . . improvement" (Middaugh, 2010, p. 93). Therefore, most of the debate around the definition of assessment revolves around its use, with more recent definitions containing references to the use of data to make changes.

While the debate continues, the basic process of assessment is that goals/outcomes are set; evidence is gathered to determine whether the goals/outcomes were met; and that evidence is reviewed and used to improve processes, systems, services and learning. What people refer to as assessment can be both context- and discipline-based. Suskie's (2004) definition of "good assessment" is one that is salient across multiple disciplines and contexts. She states that a good assessment:

- Gives us useful information.
- Gives us reasonably accurate and truthful information.
- Is fair to all students.
- Is ethical and protects the privacy and dignity of those involved.
- Is systematized.
- Is cost-effective, yielding value that justifies the time and expense involved.

The purpose of assessment has also evolved over time from an emphasis on using data for program improvements to using data to determine educational impacts on student performance, to examine program quality, and to examine institutional effectiveness.

Evaluation. The differences between evaluation and assessment have also long been debated. When Upcraft and Schuh first defined assessment in 1996, they, in turn, defined evaluation as "any effort to use assessment evidence to improve departmental, divisional or institutional effectiveness" (p. 19). In other words, evaluation was the sharing and using phase of assessment. When use of assessment data began to take prominence in the process, evaluation was interpreted as using data to make a judgment (Palomba & Banta, 1999). For many, evaluation became just a part of assessment and therefore not a distinctly different process.

Why, then, was evaluation included in the AER competency? Evaluation has different meanings for different people, often context-bound and based on use within a particular institution, discipline, or functional area. For example, the counseling center at *Institution A* may evaluate an individual client to diagnose his or her mental health but conduct an assessment on its departmental goals. The counseling center at *Institution B* may be doing the opposite, that is, assessing individuals but evaluate its services and programs. While in some contexts the two words have distinct meanings, in others they are used interchangeably and understood to mean the same thing.

Research. One thing that is widely agreed upon is that assessment and evaluation are not research. Upcraft (2003) explains that "while assessments use research methods, the central purpose of assessment differs from that of basic social science research because assessment is designed to fit different institutional and political contexts" (p. 557). The largest difference between research and assessment is purpose. Research is conducted with the intention of describing a phenomena or testing a hypothesis with the goal of adding to or confirming a knowledge base usually referred to as theory. In contrast, assessment is conducted in a specific time and place with the goal of informing practice.

Practitioners conduct assessments to inform their practice; whereas, research is conducted by researchers often disconnected from the subject that they are studying. Assessment involves the "here and now" and is meant to have immediate impact, while research focuses on long-range knowledge sharing. Assessment is driven by context while research attempts to control the context by isolating variables being studied. Research and assessment do share some common characteristics, but because of their distinctions, assessment does not need to follow the same strict methodologies that researchers follow (Timm, Barham, McKinney, & Knerr, n.d., p. 10).

Therefore, while assessment and research share some things in common such as data collection tools (surveys, focus groups, observations, etc.), data analysis techniques, and follow a cycle of inquiry; assessment and research are fundamentally different in their goals and how results are used. Keep this distinction in mind when reviewing the AER competencies. For example, if you are primarily a researcher, some outcomes under the AER competency may not apply to you, as they are specific to assessment. Alternatively, if you are primarily focused on assessment, some of the outcomes are focused on research and therefore may not be a priority.

AER Competency Levels and Rubrics

The AER competency is, like the other nine, written with three levels of proficiency: Foundational, Intermediate, and Advanced. As noted previously in this chapter, the levels are meant to guide an individual through skill development so they are not necessarily directly related to years of experience in the field. However, embedded in the AER competency are issues around political and ethical ways to use data. Upcraft (2003) once said that "All assessment is political" (p. 560). Often, navigating politics comes with experience in the field. Each of these levels is more specifically explained in the following chapters, but the descriptions below help to summarize the progression from one level to another.

Foundational Outcomes

Foundational outcomes focus on skills related to being effective consumers of research and assessment results as well as some basic elements of conducting assessment and research. The outcomes involve being able to read and interpret reports and results, apply those results, evaluate what is being presented for quality while considering how research and assessment were conducted for strengths and weaknesses, and explain processes to colleagues. Being able to evaluate research and assessment in order to determine quality is an important first step in leading these efforts. Foundational outcomes point the way to learning how to become a good consumer of information, and also focus on essential skills such as understanding confidentiality, writing outcomes and goals, communicating results clearly, and understanding research ethics.

Intermediate Outcomes

Intermediate outcomes focus on moving from being a consumer and initial participant in assessment and research to being able to independently design and implement research and assessment. These outcomes focus primarily on developing skill sets in designing processes and plans for conducting assessment and research, creating data collection tools, and managing data collection and analysis as well as accurately reporting data through various mediums. They also incorporate some nuances to research and assessment including using culturally inclusive language and processes; actively participating in assessment conversations on campus; and prioritizing projects based on goals, outcomes, or research questions.

Advanced Outcomes

Advanced outcomes guide a practitioner to a leadership role in assessment and research efforts. These outcomes are focused less on skill development and more on how one uses leadership skills. They include knowledge of politics and ethics applied to quality assessment practice at the institutional, divisional, or unit levels; creating a culture of ongoing, systematic, high quality, data-based strategies where data inform strategic planning and decision making; designing and integrating ongoing and periodic data collection efforts such that they are sustainable, rigorous, as unobtrusive as possible, and technologically current. In addition, teaching others assessment, program review, evaluation, planning, and research as to increase the likelihood of sustaining AER efforts.

ACPA/NASPA Professional Competency Rubrics

In addition to the competencies, there are ACPA/NASPA Professional Competencies Rubrics (2016). The rubric developed for AER illustrates the common elements (also known as dimensions) across all three levels and shows how a professional can progress in each of the areas (see Table 2.3).

The Assessment, Evaluation, and Research competency area focuses on the ability to design, conduct, critique, and use various AER methodologies and the results obtained from them, to utilize AER processes and their results to inform practice, and to shape the political and ethical climate surrounding AER processes and uses in higher education (ACPA & NASPA, 2015).

These common dimensions include Terms and Concepts; Values, Ethics, Politics; AER Design; Methodology, Data Collection and Data Analysis; and Interpreting, Reporting, and Using Results. When using the competencies to determine one's areas in need of development, it is important to use both the Competency Outcomes and Rubrics, as they complement one another. Like the competencies themselves, the rubrics were created with the vision that they be used in various situations such as evaluating graduate students, designing curriculums, setting and evaluating expectations between an employee and their supervisor, tracking one's own professional development, and in the design of conference and other professional development programs. While similar, the competencies and rubrics also have some slight differences.

Table 2.3
AER COMPETENCY AREA RUBRIC

	Foundational	Intermediate	Advanced
Terms and Concepts *Know and be able to describe terms, concepts, and strategies, associated with assessment, program review, evaluation, planning, and research.* *Disposition to view AER as an essential element for improvement at the unit, division, institutional, and professional levels.*	Be able to differentiate between assessment, program review, evaluation, planning, and research.	Use AER terminology consistently when participating with colleagues in assessment, program review, evaluation, planning, and research.	Lead and teach others assessment, program review, evaluation, planning, and research.
Values/Ethics/Politics *Know the value of assessment and the ethical principles associated with data collection, management, analysis, and reporting. Ability to use results towards continuous improvement; to follow institutional policies and procedures.* *Dispositions to navigate institutional politics effectively; to adhere to standards; and to sustain a culture of assessment.*	Explain institutional and divisional AER procedures and policies with regard to ethical assessment, evaluation, and other research activities. Identify political and educational sensitivity of raw and partially processed data and AER results. Handle data with appropriate confidentiality and deference to organizational hierarchies.	Contribute actively to the development of a culture of evidence at the department level by providing AER training, advocating for funding, and incorporating AER in practice. Manage and/or adhere to the implementation of institutional and professional standards for ethical AER activities. Use culturally relevant and appropriate terms and methods to conduct and report AER findings.	Create a culture of evidence in which AER is central to practice and in which training happens across the organization. Ensure institutional, divisional, or unit compliance with professional ethical standards concerning AER activities. Anticipate and respond to challenges related to individual and institutional politics, competing constituencies and interests, and divergent values.

continued

Table 2.3—*Continued*

	Foundational	Intermediate	Advanced
AER Design			
Know theoretical frameworks that align with organizational outcomes, goals, and values. Ability to create learner-centered outcomes that align with divisional and institutional priorities; ability to design and lead a process-oriented strategy to address the assessment's purpose or research questions. *Disposition to think critically and systematically about questions and problems of practice.*	Design program and learning outcomes that are clear, specific, and measurable; and which informed by theoretical frameworks and aligned with organizational outcomes, goals, and values. Utilize theoretical frameworks and organizational outcomes, goals, and values to design program and learning outcomes. Explain to students and colleagues the relationship of AER processes to learning outcomes and goals.	Prioritize program and learning outcomes with organization's goals and values. Utilize student learning and development theories and scholarly research to inform content and design of learning outcomes and assessment tools. Educate stakeholders about the relationship of departmental AER processes to learning outcomes and goals at the student, department, division, and institutional level. Discern appropriate design(s) based on critical questions, available data, and intended audience(s).	Lead the conceptualization and design of ongoing, systematic, high-quality, data-based strategies at the institutional, divisional, and/or unit-wide level to evaluate and assess learning; programs, services, and personnel. Use assessment and evaluation results in determining institutional, divisional or unit accomplishments toward mission/goals, reallocation of resources, and advocacy for more resources. Lead a comprehensive communication process to inform campus stakeholders about the relationship of AER processes to learning outcomes, and goals at the student, department, division, and institution level.

continued

Table 2.3—*Continued*

	Foundational	*Intermediate*	*Advanced*
Methodology, Data Collection, and Data Analysis *Know strengths and limits of research methodologies. Ability to match methodology with purpose of assessment and guiding questions; to collect and analyze data.* *Dispositions to take a critical stance in collection and analysis of data; rigorous attention to detail; creative thinking.*	Differentiate among methods for assessment, program review, evaluation, planning, and research. Facilitate data collection for system/department-wide assessment and evaluation efforts using current technology and methods. Assess trustworthiness, and/or validity of studies of various methods and methodological designs. Consider strengths and limitations of methodological approaches when applying findings to practice in diverse institutional settings and with diverse student populations.	Design data collection efforts that are ongoing, sustainable, rigorous, unobtrusive, and technologically current. Demonstrate working knowledge of alternative methodological AER approaches and strategies for ensuring quality results. Participate in the design of qualitative and quantitative AER projects, determining appropriate methods and analyses for each. Articulate the limitations of findings imposed by differences in how quantitative and qualitative data are sampled, analyzed, and verified through validity, reliability, and/or trustworthiness techniques.	Design and integrate ongoing and periodic data collection efforts such that they are sustainable, rigorous, as unobtrusive as possible, and technologically current. Lead, supervise, and/or collaborate with others to design and analyze assessment, program review, evaluation, and research activities that span multiple methodological approaches.

continued

Table 2.3—*Continued*

	Foundational	Intermediate	Advanced
Interpreting, Reporting, and Using Results *Know how to interpret data in practical terms that are relevant to the institutional context. Ability to present results concisely in reports that are useful to a variety of audiences; ability to use findings to make informed decisions and to align resources.* *Dispositions to collaborate; to represent findings accurately and fairly; to share interpretations with stakeholders, including students.*	Articulate, interpret, and apply results of AER reports and studies, including professional literature. Ensure all communications of AER results are accurate, responsible, and effective.	Effectively manage, align, and guide the utilization of AER reports and studies. Communicate and display data in a manner that is accurate, transparent about the strengths, limitations, and context of the data; and sensitive to political coalitions and realities associated with data as a scarce resource. Effectively use assessment and evaluation results in determining the institution's, the division's, or the unit's accomplishment of its missions/goals, reallocation of resources, and advocacy for more resources.	Lead the design and writing of varied and diverse communications of assessment, program review, evaluation, and other research activities that include translation of data analysis into goals and action. Write and disseminate results in a manner that critically considers the strengths and limitations of implications for practice, policy, theory, and/or future study in a sophisticated way. Integrate the strategic use and prioritization of budgetary and personnel resources to support high-quality program evaluation, assessment efforts, research, and planning. Facilitate the prioritization of decisions and resources to implement those decisions that are informed by AER activities.

The original outcomes published in the source document (ACPA/ NASPA Professional Competency Areas of Student Affairs Educators, 2015) did not always develop across all levels of mastery. For example, a foundational outcome might "disappear," failing to continue across subsequent levels of mastery. Conversely, some outcomes "appeared" in the intermediate or advanced levels without an origin in the foundational level (ACPA/NASPA Professional Competency Rubrics, 2016, p. 9).

While these two documents complement one another, they are not exactly aligned; therefore, it is important to consult both documents when determining potential areas of development.

At the foundational level, many of the outcomes in AER focus on understanding and applying concepts and terminology. Before moving on to other chapters in this book, which explore each outcome more deeply, it is important to become familiar with words and phrases used in assessment and throughout the rubrics and competencies. These are also words and phrases you will encounter in subsequent chapters. Definitions are included so that you will have a reference guide as you explore the AER competency more deeply. The terms were chosen

Table 2.4
TERMS AND CONCEPTS

	Foundational	*Intermediate*	*Advanced*
Terms and Concepts *Know and be able to describe terms, concepts, and strategies associated with assessment, program review, evaluation, planning and research.* *Disposition to view AER as an essential element for improvement at the unit, division, institutional, and professional levels.*	Be able to differentiate between assessment, program review, evaluation, planning, and research.	Use AER terminology consistently when participating with colleagues in assessment, program review, evaluation, planning, and research.	Lead and teach others assessment, program review, evaluation, planning, and research.

based on what someone new to AER may find helpful, but the list is not exhaustive. If you come across a term not on this list, conducting a web search on the term or looking at a reliable website can be very helpful.

Anonymity: Anonymity is guaranteed when neither the researcher nor the readers of the findings can identify a given response with a given respondent (Babbie & Mouton, 2001).

Benchmark: An internal or external standard used to compare assessment findings. It is the measurement of individual or group performance against an established standard.

Bias: Bias occurs when the measurement or sample is influenced in such a way that conclusions from data may be flawed. See also the definitions for biased sample and measurement bias (Weinbach & Grinnell, 2001).

Biased sample: Biased sample means that a sample is selected in such a way that some members of the population are more likely than others to be picked for sample membership (Weinbach & Grinnell, 2001).

Causality: When changes in one variable are caused by changes in another variable, the relationship is considered causal.

Cocurricular: Cocurricular refers to activities, programs, and learning experiences that complement or mirror, in some way, what students are learning in the classroom. Cocurricular learning activities are typically, but not always, defined by their separation from academic courses (Great Schools Partnership, 2013).

Cognitive/noncognitive skills: Cognitive skills focus on intellectual effort, such as thinking, reasoning, or remembering. Noncognitive skills are related to motivation, integrity, and interpersonal interaction. They may also involve intellect, but more indirectly and less consciously than cognitive skills (ACT, n.d.).

Confirmatory: Typically, confirmatory refers to confirming findings. This process differs for quantitative versus qualitative methods.

Closing the loop: Closing the loop in the cycle of assessment moves from defining mission and objectives to using assessment results for program change and improvement.

Confidentiality: Confidentiality is guaranteed when the researcher can identify a given person's responses but promises not to do so publicly (Babbie & Mouton, 2001).

Confounding variables: Confounding variables are factors outside of the observed independent variables that could explain changes or differences in the dependent variable. For example, if we observed that participants in the residence life program had higher feelings of social belonging than those who didn't, the results could also be explained by pre-existing differences in social belonging. If students who were already very socially engaged felt more comfortable attending a residence life program, the post-program differences would be confounded by preprogram social belonging.

Content validity "ensures the instrument is measuring the breadth and depth of the issue that it is intended to measure" (Lodico, Spaulding, & Voegtle, 2006, p. 112). When conducting research, content validity is usually tested during the pilot-testing process. If a pilot does not occur, then a second option is to have the instrument reviewed by a peer who has specialized knowledge in the topic to determine if it is leaving out any important questions related to the topic and if questions included on the survey are appropriately related to the topic.

Continuous improvement: Continuous improvement derives from efforts to use data towards improvement of products, services, or processes.

Control variables: A control variable is one that is held constant. Control variables can be addressed through both the design of a study and in the examination of results.

Correlation: Correlation is a measure of the degree of association between two variables without assuming any causality.

Culture of assessment: Culture of assessment is an environment in which continuous improvement through the collection and use of assessment is expected and valued.

Culture of evidence: Culture of evidence is a commitment to show through data how programs, processes, and products are effective and fulfill larger initiatives and goals.

Data analysis: Data analysis involves the process of transforming raw data into usable information, in order to add value to the statistical output.

Dependent variable: The dependent variable is the factor the researcher hopes to change or influence through some process.

Ethnographic study: Deriving from ethnographic research, it is a type of qualitative method in which researchers completely immerse themselves in the lives, culture, or situation they are studying. They are often lengthy studies.

Experimental design: In an experimental design, the researcher manipulates the independent variable(s) to determine its effect on some behavior or cognitive process (the dependent variable). Random assignment of participants to groups control external factors from influencing the results.

Face validity: Face validity if the instrument appears to be measuring what it purports to measure. This means that on the surface, the questions seem to fit whatever is the described purpose of the instrument (Lodico et al., 2006). Face validity can be determined through a pilot-test of an instrument, or by asking peers with knowledge of the purpose and instrument design to provide a review of the instrument.

Generalize (generalizability): Generalizability is the degree to which results from a particular study can be generalized to other participants or other situations. It is the process in testing and statistics theory that takes a score from a sample of behaviors and applies them to the entire possible set of observations.

Goals: Comprehensive statements that may reflect the broad, overarching, long-range intentions of the division or department (Bresciani, 2010).

Independent variable: Independent variables, unlike dependent variables, are not influenced by what the researcher does. The researcher has complete control over the selection of independent variables and selects one believed to impact the dependent (outcome) variables.

Institutional Review Board: An Institutional Review Board (IRB) at each college or university reviews assessment, research, and research proposals before they are conducted to ensure that participants are protected from physical or psychological harm. This includes ensuring that data will be kept confidential, participants will not be coerced into participating, and questions being asked do not pose a risk to participants. IRB approval is required for any AER studies if findings will be published or used outside the institutional context.

Learning outcomes: Learning outcomes are changes in students' knowledge, skills, attitudes, and habits of mind that result from involvement in a program, event, or activity. It describes what you want the student to know and do. Outcomes are statements of what you will assess.

Limitations: Limitations are influences to assessment, evaluation, and research that are not in the researcher's control. These can place restrictions on methodology and conclusions, and as such must be acknowledged to assist the reader in interpreting findings.

Longitudinal data: A longitudinal study design involves the collection of data at different points in time to determine trends (Babbie & Mouton, 2001).

Measurement: Measurement refers to the methods used to gather information, typically using quantitative, qualitative, or mixed methods approaches.

Measurement bias: Measurement bias is a systematic source of measurement distortion that can occur because of a wide variety of phenomenon. For example, measurement bias may occur if an interviewer unconsciously skews how they ask questions depending on the subject or if a survey is sent out during an atypical time of the year (Weinbach & Grinnell, 2001).

Methodologies: Different and distinct from "methods" (see below); methodology explains, "Why you have chosen to do your research in the way that you have chosen" (Thomas, 2013, p. 30). This includes explaining the choice of research question, and approaches to gather data to explore that question. Often this is done through drawing on the literature reviewed and is also based on one's philosophical stance (also known as positivist or interpretivist stance). Positivists believe that knowledge is objective and therefore is observable, measurable, and can be studied scientifically; whereas, interpretivists believe that knowledge is constructed by our perceived worlds and our context. Therefore, knowledge is about interpreting the expressed views and behaviors of others. Understanding and explaining to others what broad methodology you are using when conducting research from helps define your choices as a researcher (Thomas, 2013).

Methods: A tool used to collect data related to an assessment or research project. Data collection tools can range from surveys, focus groups, observations, rubrics, interviews, document analysis, and many other options (Yousey-Elsener, 2014).

Mission statement: Describes the broad, shared purpose and vision of the organization. A college or university will have mission statements at multiple levels and alignment is extremely important.

Mixed methods: Mixed methods are procedures for collecting both qualitative and quantitative data in a single study. Mixing both quantitative and qualitative research and data allows for greater breadth and depth of understanding.

Nonfindings: In statistical testing, nonfindings refer to nonsignificant results.

Outcomes: Outcomes essentially take an objective and bound it to a place, time, group of participants, and a level for performance. Outcomes identify what you want the end result of programming efforts to be, the changes you want to occur. Outcomes are statements of what you will assess.

Practical significance (see also statistical significance): When sample sizes are very large (over 1,000) or very small (less than 100), data may show a statistical significance with the slightest difference between groups. In these cases, it is important to ask a larger question about whether the finding is practically significant or whether the differences are meaningful in specific context. Data can be practically significant without being statistically significant as well as the opposite—statistically significant but not practically significant. For example, a campus may find that statistical significance reported on a national benchmarking survey is not practically significant because it does not apply to the mission or priorities of the campus (Yousey-Elsener, 2013, p. 144).

Program or operational outcomes: "Describe how a program, course, or operation will change as a result of a planned course of action" (Yousey-Elsener, 2013, p. 143). They often set expectations around efficiency, effectiveness, climate, needs, and/or satisfaction.

Program review: "Program review is a comprehensive evaluation of an academic/administrative program or department that is designed both to foster improvement and demonstrate accountability. Program reviews typically include a self-study conducted by the program's faculty and staff, a visit by one or more external reviewers, and recommendations for improvement based on the conclusions of the self-study and the reviewer" (Suskie, 2009, p. 14).

Qualitative data: These are ways of collecting information concerned with understanding or conveying meaning or contexts, rather than making statistical inferences. "The detailed descriptions of situations, events, people, interactions, and observed behaviors; use of direct quotations from people about their experiences, attitudes, beliefs, and thoughts; and analysis of excerpts or entire passages from documents, correspondences, records and case histories" (Upcraft & Schuh, 1996, p. 21).

Quantitative data: The assignment of numbers to objects, events, or observations according to some rule for the purposes of statistical analysis (Upcraft & Schuh, 1996).

Quasi-experiment (see experimental design): A quasi-experimental design is similar to an experimental design but without random assignment.

Random assignment: Random assignment is a procedure in experiments that ensures that each participant has an equal opportunity to be assigned to any given group. In a study, participants are randomly assigned to different groups, such as the experimental or control group. This helps to ensure that any differences between and within the groups are not systematic at the outset of the experiment.

Raw data: Raw data is data in its original form, as collected, before interpretation using qualitative or quantitative methods.

Reliability: Reliability deals with the extent to which an assessment tool provides stable and consistent results across assessment occasions and internal to the assessment. Reliability indices include test-retest reliability, parallel forms reliability, inter-rater reliability, and internal consistency reliability. Reliability is the consistency of measurement, or the degree to which an instrument measures the same way each time it is used under the same condition with the same subjects. In short, it is the repeatability of a measurement. A measure is considered reliable if a person's score on the same test given twice is similar.

Rubric: "Rubric is a scoring guide usually in the form of a list or chart that describes the criteria that will be used to evaluate a document, object, or demonstrated performance (e.g., mock interview, role-play, oral presentation)" (Suskie, 2009, p. 137–138).

Sample (sampling): A sample is a subgroup of a population selected to participate in an activity, program, or service. The results from the sample are used to generalize to the larger population from which the sample was drawn. There are many different types of sampling methods; for example, simple random, stratified sampling, cluster sampling, to name a few.

Stakeholder: A person, group or organization, internal or external to an organization, that has interest or concern in an organization. Stakeholders can affect or be affected by the organization's actions, objectives, and policies.

Statistical significance (see also practical significance): Statistical tests allow the researcher to make decisions about the data.

Statistical significance is expressed in terms of probability. Probability is a number that describes the likely occurrence of a particular event. Therefore, tests of statistical significance tell us the likelihood of something happening by chance or as a result of what was being done as part of the research project or assessment (Thomas, 2013).

Strategic planning: Strategic planning refers to the process in which organizations engage in reviewing their mission statement and goals, and then designing and adopting action steps to achieve their goals (Schuh & Associates, 2009).

Transparency/systematic: Depending on the context these two words can have different or similar meanings. Suskie (2004) defines good assessment as systematized. And researchers are sometimes called upon to explain the systems they used to collect and analyze data. While these concepts may seem different, they are similar and both involve being able to explain to others why you are asking the questions you are asking (research), why you are exploring the outcomes you set (assessment), why/when/how you are collecting data, etc. Transparency also includes sharing results and closing the assessment loop by using findings to address goals and intended outcomes. Transparent is often coupled with systematic because it is the act of being upfront and explaining why you are doing what you have planned so that others can know and understand your work.

Trustworthiness: Researchers differ a great deal in the language they use to describe the process of assessing the internal validity (accuracy), the external validity (generalizability), and reliability (consistency, replicability) of a qualitative study. Lincoln and Guba (1985) refer to the "trustworthiness" of qualitative research and use terms such as "credibility," "transferability," and "dependability," and "confirmability." Credibility deals with the accuracy of identifying and describing the subject of the study; transferability deals with the applicability of the findings to another context; dependability is the researcher's account of the changes inherent in any setting as well as changes to the research design as learning unfolded; and confirmability deals with whether the findings could be confirmed by another researcher, thus removing some of the researcher subjectivity.

Validity: Addresses the question: Does the instrument used measure what it is intended to measure? There are statistical tests that can be run to measure validity, but they require a large data set. For smaller datasets, we focus on face validity and content validity (see definitions).

Conclusion

The remaining chapters in this book explore each of the dimensions in the AER rubric, including an in-depth look into what competency may look like at various levels, how to apply the competency, a chance to experience that dimension through a case study, and self-assessment to determine one's areas that need to be strengthened and developed. Below are examples of student learning outcomes, a self-reflection chart and guiding statements that will assist you with further understanding the content in this chapter.

Teacher's Assessment of Student
The student should be able to:
1. Articulate the two functions served by the competency levels: foundational, intermediate, and advanced levels under each competency.
2. Articulate the differences and similarities between assessment, evaluation, and research.

Student Self-reflection
For this self-reflection exercise, you are provided with questions to check your own understanding.
1. How would you explain the ACPA/NASPA Professional Competencies to someone? How might they be used for someone at your level?
2. After looking at the description of the 10 competencies, where are your areas of strength? What areas do you need to develop?

continued

3. How would you describe the similarities and differences between assessment, evaluation, and research? Describe an example of each of these.

4. Why are skills in assessment, evaluation, and research important for student affairs professionals? How might they be used in a professional's daily activities?

Author's Reponses to Student Self-Reflection

1. How would you explain the ACPA/NASPA Professional Competencies to someone? How might they be used for someone at your level? *ACPA/NASPA Professional Competencies help people working as college administrators to evaluate their skills sets and figure out areas of improvement. As these skills sets need development over time, the Professional Competencies can help someone identify gaps or areas where they have particularly excelled. Someone can use them for a self-assessment, supervisors could use them to help develop the people they supervise, and graduate programs/conference planners/etc. can use them to structure curriculum.*

2. After looking at the description of the 10 competencies, where are your areas of strength? What areas do you need to develop? *For example: Looking at the descriptions of the 10 competencies, I would consider my top strengths in the areas of Assessment, Evaluation and Research; Advising and Supporting; Personal and Ethical Foundations; Organizational and Human Resources. While I feel like I know the basics in all of the areas, the four areas where I could use more in-depth development are Law, Policy, and Governance; Social Justice and Inclusion; Technology; and Leadership.*

3. How would you describe the similarities and differences between assessment, evaluation, and research? Describe an example of each of these. *All three are similar in that they involve identifying goals, gathering information (aka data), and using that information to make a change or improvement. They differ in their purpose, with assessment and evaluation being more practice-based, context driven, and meant to have an effect on individuals, groups, or office/systems. Research, on the other hand, is meant to contribute to a larger body of knowledge and applies to a broader audience than assessment and evaluation.*

4. Why are skills in assessment, evaluation, and research important for student affairs professionals? How might they be used in a professional's daily activities? *AER skills help professionals learn more about the impact they are having on students and other constituencies. Whether they are trying to learn more about how helpful their services are, what students are learning, how they can better use resources, or how efficient their processes are, strong AER skills help professionals gather useful information in order to be more informed about what they are doing and make changes that have a positive impact on their areas. In addition, AER skills help professionals gather information that is useful to others at the institution and, if data are collected wisely, can inform larger conversations on campus. Stronger skills prepare professionals to be a part of these conversations.*

Chapter 3

STUDENT AFFAIRS ASSESSMENT IN THE BROADER INSTITUTIONAL CONTEXT: VALUES, ETHICS, AND POLITICS

LANCE C. KENNEDY-PHILLIPS AND LEAH EWING ROSS

The promise of higher education, and the expectations that result, are substantial. There is an implicit belief in our society that an educated citizenry is an essential component of healthy communities, a strong workforce, and a productive economy. Understandably, stakeholders want evidence of return on their investment, which proves challenging beyond documenting success in the most tangible ways, such as measuring retention and degree production. We know that students' academic pursuits are affected by their experiences outside of the classroom, but to date, we have struggled to clearly define return on investment in this arena. It is not enough to point to evidence of overall institutional success and simply claim that student affairs programs contribute to those gains or to assert that the benefits of participation in extracurricular programs are not measurable.

Although it may seem daunting for student affairs units to "tell our stories" through data and information of the impact we have, it is our responsibility and our ethical obligation. Tapping into the passion we share for higher education and student success allows us to craft narratives that draw connections between institutions' missions, program goals, and students' needs, and bring those connections to life with solid evidence of accomplishment and responsible stewardship of resources. As such, meeting demands for accountability is a germane part of our work.

This chapter explores the impact of the accountability movement through the lenses of values, ethics, and politics—considered collectively as a culture of evidence. We start with reflection on the student affairs reality and consider the role of assessment as part of a culture of evidence. The increased focus on ethics in assessment of student learning runs parallel to growing demands for accountability in American higher education overall, and subsequent expectations that every institutional division and unit—including student affairs—have data available on-demand, at all times. We weave the topics of this chapter together, culminating in our overarching assertion that in order to fully answer the call to build and sustain a culture of evidence, each of us needs to learn as much as we can about our institutions overall and develop understandings of the various political contexts at play. To do so, we must build networks with colleagues in other units and divisions, learn where pockets of expertise exist, and identify opportunities to collaborate.

The Student Affairs Reality

Historically, faculty members have been charged with the "learning" side of the academic enterprise, and student affairs professionals were relegated to planning fun activities to keep students busy when they were not in class or studying. That is not the world in which we live anymore; that era passed long ago, and it is important for students to share responsibility for their learning and success. Gansemer-Topf and Kennedy-Phillips (2017) explained that "student learning takes place at the intersection of three factors: the curricular environment, the cocurricular environment, and the student's motivation. Colleges and universities must be able to demonstrate that student learning occurs at this intersection and that all actors—academic affairs divisions, student affairs divisions, and students—are contributing to the learning process" (p. 331).

Academic and student affairs professionals must have access to sound and reliable data to tell our stories, to exhibit a clear understanding of institutional needs, to maintain clearly defined goals for programs and services, and to assure rigorous assessment practices that provide solid evidence of accomplishment. Colleges and universities across the country have had to devise new methods of telling our stories to our communities, because these practices are relatively new for many organizations.

In many cases, the challenges are for student affairs programs to demonstrate fulfillment of the academic missions of our institutions and the holistic development of students, and simultaneously demonstrate responsible stewardship of institutional resources. The creation and maintenance of cultures of evidence built on consistent and meaningful data collection provide the foundation for student affairs divisions to assess our contributions to completing the educational mission of any institution. A strong and sustained culture of evidence demonstrates how resources are used appropriately to support the necessary functions of our organizations.

Shifts in Understanding Student Learning

There has been a shift in the paradigm that once influenced higher education. Historically, faculty presented information, and *students* had the responsibility to learn. Furthermore, it was believed that most learning—or the most important learning—occurred in the classroom. Yet as Woodard, Love, and Komives (2000) explained, "it is simplistic to think that the curriculum is the realm of learning, and the cocurriculum is the realm of personal development. Learning and development are integrated, symbiotic processes" (pp. 50–51). Outcomes-based assessment changed the way teaching and learning are constructed. To address this new paradigm, higher education professionals started asking pointed questions, such as: How do we know we are effective? How can we quantify and qualify that we provide students what we promised them when they enrolled? What evidence demonstrates that students achieve desired learning outcomes?

Through outcomes assessment, we have learned that it is not enough for everyone involved in the higher education enterprise to focus on individual interests, even if independently we achieve our intended outcomes. Rather, we need to come together—faculty, administrators, *and students*—to make sure that student learning happens in a systemic and integrated manner. Barr and Tagg (1995) described this as part of the Learning Paradigm, in which "a college's purpose is not to transfer knowledge but to create environments and experiences that bring students to discover and construct knowledge for themselves, to make students members of communities of learners that make discoveries and solve problems" (p. 15). Learning takes place both in and out of the classroom; however, student affairs professionals need to do a better job of teaching students how to be active and engaged learners in nontraditional and informal learning spaces.

The current understanding of learning in higher education does not emphasize a curricular/cocurricular dichotomy (as was true in the past); in fact, the curricular/co-curricular interdependence is now understood and accepted as a given. Student learners choose to engage and get involved in their institutional communities (or not); they bring their past and present experiences to the classroom, take lessons learned in the classroom to situations and experiences out of the classroom, and vice versa. As such, three aspects form the triad of the ultimate teachable moment: student learner motivation, the formal curriculum, and the cocurriculum. The culmination of these concepts results in well-rounded and successful participants of our society, our communities, and the economy (Oaks, 2015).

Literature provides a strong foundation for our understanding in this area. Nearly three decades ago, Lave and Wenger (1991) posited that learning is embedded in, and cannot be isolated from, its physical and social environments or its social coconstruction. In essence, learning does not occur in a vacuum. Around the same time, Baxter Magolda (1992) explained that "situating learning in the students' own experience legitimizes their knowledge as a foundation for constructing new knowledge" (p. 378). Later, *Learning Reconsidered* (Keeling, 2004) defined learning as "a comprehensive, holistic, transformative activity that integrates academic learning and student development, processes that have often been considered separate, and even independent of each other" (p. 2).

This shift in the higher education community's approach to learning was summarized by Suskie (2015):

> The last two generations have seen a revolution in American higher education. One facet of this revolution is the transformation of out-of-classroom experiences from activities that students simply enjoy to experiences in which students also learn important things. . . . Another facet of this revolution is the move from . . . a culture of anecdotes to a culture of evidence. (p. 5)

Stewardship of Institutional Resources

While it is important to acknowledge the role student affairs plays in learning and development, it is equally important for those in the

profession to focus on appropriate stewardship of institutional resources. A strong and sustained culture of evidence demonstrates how
resources are appropriately allocated, and how those resources support the necessary functions of student affairs divisions.

Think of a coin. On one side of the coin is the need to show that
student affairs professionals are active partners in the institution's
learning enterprise. We develop programs with increased intentionality toward student learning and the ultimate goal of creating transformational experiences for students. We need to demonstrate how our
work contributes to teaching and learning in a twenty-first century
context, which means education that utilizes both curricular and
cocurricular high-impact practices (HIPs) and emphasizes the development of transferable skills and increased competencies. The other
side of the coin is the stewardship of institutional resources, which in
some cases includes budgets that span hundreds of thousands or even
millions of dollars. As such, there is a need for sound data to demonstrate how funds are spent and what goals are achieved as a result.

An effective student affairs organization measures progress toward
mission fulfillment and accomplishment of strategic goals at all levels.
The data and information collected through a sound assessment and
research process is evidence. A robust body of evidence is necessary
for an organization to grow and improve. For example, simply measuring occupancy in university housing with data pulled from a student information system does not provide a full picture of the impact
of the residential experience on student success. If we are going to
leverage information to convey the most effective stories, sound and
rigorous data collection and analyses must be priorities. This is
achieved through the institution's commitment to assessment.

The Value of Assessment

Assessment takes place at many levels—institutional, divisional, departmental, programmatic, and more. The *doing* of assessment is important (collecting and analyzing data), but the value is in use of the
information produced. That is, a culture of assessment is an essential
component of a culture of evidence, which cannot be sustained if
information is not used. Yet, using information requires data and information literacy on the part of the individuals who engage in the work
of assessment (producers), and those who use the results for decision
making (consumers) (Ross & Lewis, 2017).

A culture of evidence, use of information, and information literacy requires institutional *and* individual commitment. Realization of these concepts is heavily dependent on support from senior leadership and the allocation of resources. Most of us will experience a wide variety of environments throughout our careers in which this work is valued more or less, yet our commitment at the individual level should not waiver. Assessment touches the core of higher education in that it focuses on improvement in support of student success. Higher education professionals must use that as a touchstone, regardless of our specific roles, responsibilities, and the climates in which we work.

The ways in which individual professionals contribute to cultures of evidence can be explored through engagement with the pillars of data-informed decision cultures—data quality, transparency, and data use—which ensure that "cultures are actionable, relatable to institutions' missions and goals, and grounded within the larger context of higher education" (Ross & Lewis, 2017, p. 2). For the purposes of this chapter, the terms *data-informed decision culture* and *data* are synonymous with the terms *culture of evidence* and *information.*

Individual commitment to the pillars of data quality, transparency, and data use ensures the integrity of our work, and contributes to the realization of a culture of evidence at every level of the organization. The context for this work varies; that is, it may look and feel different by department, division, or institution, but "the essence of the culture is collaboration in pursuit of the institution's goals; simply put, silos and 'turf wars' are minimized or eliminated. A collegial environment lends itself to dynamic use of data, timely feedback loops, and continued investment in data quality and transparency" (Ross & Lewis, 2017, p. 2). The mere existence and availability of information does not automatically result in use or in appropriate use. It is possible for data and information to be accurate but not relevant. Information is only valuable if it answers the questions posed. Information that is not valuable is not used, or worse, results in inaccurate or inappropriate interpretations. Data quality and context matter.

Data and Information Quality

A culture of evidence relies on information quality. Much of the work of assessment is devoted to ensuring accuracy; this includes vetting the credibility of data collection methods, ensuring sound analyses, and contextualizing interpretations. Each process involves use of established protocols. As a result, some assessment professionals hesitate to make data widely available to others because when control is forfeited, accuracy can be compromised, and interpretations can be incorrect. Yet as Ross and Lewis (2017) explained, "this restrictive approach can result in lower quality data" (p. 2). That is, when data are provided to a wide array of stakeholders, people use them and become invested in data quality. As a wider array of stakeholders becomes interested in the information available and the work at hand, communication increases and silos are minimized.

Furthermore, there is greater investment in quality when data literacy expands among both consumers and producers. It is impossible to grow data literacy without communication, guidance, and trust, all of which assessment professionals foster through collaboration with individuals in other offices and units. Accountability is not abandoned when data and information are shared. Evidence of validity and reliability is always of utmost importance, regardless of how information is used and who uses it.

Each of us has a responsibility to ensure the quality of data and information. Do not confuse a commitment to quality with expectations that all student affairs professionals be data scientists or assessment experts. Rather, ensuring data quality necessitates attention to detail and an understanding of context in order to interpret and apply information appropriately, identify and address mistakes, and answer the questions at hand. This requires both consumers' and producers' participation.

Transparency

In assessment, transparency is realized when initiatives are designed for the purpose of exploration and not with the sole intent of showcasing program success. Furthermore, assessment results must be available in full to achieve transparency. Summaries and reports are crafted to answer pertinent questions for relevant audiences, of course, but that does not mean that less desirable information is concealed or misrepresented.

Also, attention should be paid to transparency with both internal and external stakeholders. All members of the institutional community are decision makers—including administrators, staff, faculty, and students—and they require timely access to relevant information (Swing & Ross, 2016b). External audiences are often less familiar with higher education vernacular and the details of programs and services, and therefore to achieve transparency in communication of study results, explicit "articulation of accomplishments and need, including the provision of relevant data and information in formats that are easy to consume" is required (Ross & Lewis, 2017, p. 2). This does not mean that "providing more data to more people" automatically results in transparency (Ross & Lewis, p. 3). Rather, it is essential to understand the audience and provide the information needed in a consumable format without intentionally or unintentionally obfuscating transparency.

Trust does not exist without a commitment to transparency. "Stakeholders need to know what is happening and why, and it is with transparency—access, communication, and accountability—that trust is established and commitment from relevant parties is garnered and sustained" (Ross & Lewis, 2017, p. 2). Transparency must be maintained in times of success *and* times of challenge; that is, trust is established when a program, unit, or institution is transparent in light of mistakes and unattained goals. This is easier said than done, of course, especially when there is pressure to make things "look good," and when the allocation of resources is linked to evidence of success. However, if we maintain focus on the overarching goal of supporting and improving student success, the importance of transparency is never out of focus.

Just as with the quality of data and information, transparency cannot be achieved and sustained without everyone's commitment; it is not the sole responsibility of data experts and communications officers. All higher education professionals, regardless of scopes of responsibility, should document the processes we employ and be able to articulate the intent of our work and identify how relevant goals are achieved and measured. Transparency happens on small and large scales, and the need for it permeates the institution from every angle, thereby engaging all of us in efforts to build and sustain atmospheres of trust.

Ethical Codes of Conduct

There are numerous ethical codes of conduct that guide the assessment professional's work, including, but not limited to, statements provided by the American Educational Research Association (2011), Association for Institutional Research (2013), Council for the Advancement of Standards in Higher Education (2015), discipline-specific organizations, and institutional policies. The ethics statements address expectations and requirements for accuracy, honesty, integrity, and responsibility, and include guidance for situations in which violations of these key principles occur. Although ethical conduct applies to all aspects of a higher education professional's work, transparency helps ensure that accuracy, honesty, and integrity are maintained. Lack of transparency raises ethical concerns. Without each member of the community's commitment to transparency, it cannot be sustained. Collaboration and communication within units and across the institution are the only ways to fully realize transparency. Simply put, we must each do our part.

Data and Information Use

If the information garnered through assessment is not used, the keys to creating a culture of assessment—relevance, intentionality, sustainability, and authenticity—are not realized. It is through the collective efforts of assessment professionals in particular, and the higher education community overall, that a culture of assessment is achieved and sustained in support of a culture of evidence. In turn, institutions that realize robust cultures of evidence commit to the use of data in decision making at all levels, by all members of the community and all stakeholders, both internal and external (Ross & Lewis, 2017). This requires each of us to commit to the use of data and information in our work, to support others' use, and to recognize an expanded definition of decision makers (Swing & Ross, 2016b).

Creating a Culture of Evidence

Creating a culture of evidence requires all members of the higher education enterprise to ensure that our work is relevant, intentional, sustainable, and authentic.

Relevance

A strong culture of evidence reflects the values, mission, and vision of the institution. It injects timely, useful, and reliable evidence into all levels of the institution's decision-making process. Development of a culture of evidence requires honest and transparent discussion about the current environment. Without this context, it is difficult to establish relevance, and without relevance, it is nearly impossible to sustain programs and services.

The challenge here for student affairs is particularly high because many cocurricular experiences are labor-intensive, and therefore relatively expensive. Sustainable programs clearly demonstrate that they are cost-effective; directly related to the institution's values, mission, and vision; and that students achieve identified goals. The cost of some cocurricular experiences is relatively easy to justify. Programs designed to increase student retention, for example, can benchmark their costs against tuition revenue from retained students. For other programs, however, comparing costs and impact is more difficult.

As higher education professionals, our work should be guided by the values of the organization and the institutions for which we work. There will be times when questions arise about the relevance of a project or task. That is when the following question should be posed: Do I see the mission and values of the organization in the work I am doing? This simple question never loses significance and should the guide the work of new professionals and senior administrators alike.

Intentionality

To fulfill its mission, an institution needs to create optimal learning environments for students. Internal and external stakeholders expect the institution to use data to inform those efforts and to measure their worth. Intentionality is the use of data and information to ensure that a culture of evidence promotes continuous improvement of the institution and fosters transparency. We define an intentional student affairs organization as one that is outcomes-focused, data-driven, reflective, and open to change.

The essential premise of assessment is to move programs and initiatives from "what we would like to do" to "what needs to be done." We contend, however, that assessment should always be motivated by self-improvement so that it moves from being merely reactionary (accountability only) to being truly transformative in the delivery of programs and services focused on student success.

As student affairs administrators realize a need to collect research and assessment data, questions emerge about how best to use that information to guide program improvement. Some efforts prioritize the use of information to align programs with institutional priorities, and others seek to demonstrate the impact of cocurricular activities on student learning. However, a growing trend is to use data to tell all of the institution's stories—compelling narratives about students' experiences, program success, and realization of the institution's goals.

Intentionality may seem simple as a concept, but can be very difficult in practice. For example, it is of utmost importance that we not affect change for the sake of change; without intentionality, change devalues assessment efforts. To demonstrate intentionality, a student affairs professional should be able to produce evidence to support any suggestions for change. We often are caught believing change shows progress, when in fact, we can do the student affairs organization or the institution more harm by affecting change without intentionality than by not changing at all.

Sustainability

Sustainability comes in many forms for an institution, as discussed later in this chapter. A sustainable culture of evidence involves regular reviews of institutional policies and procedures supported by data and information; use of evidence in balance with institutional history to reinforce standards and values; and institutional commitment to the creation of the infrastructure, tools, and training required to support data-informed decision making.

All student affairs divisions should develop sustainable cultures of evidence to support decision-making processes. The accountability movement has become an important consideration for all levels of management and leadership in American higher education. "Parents, legislators, employers, and students want assurances that the higher education environment is a pathway to employment on graduation. They want to believe that the university is providing students with the skills they need to be successful in their career pursuits and as citizens in a global society (Gansemer-Topf & Kennedy-Phillips, 2017, p. 331).

Professionals at every level of the student affairs organization must be involved to sustain a culture of evidence. Senior leaders need to demonstrate commitment publicly and behind the scenes. Mid-level professionals need to coach and develop new professionals to help them understand their roles in achieving the goals of the institution overall, and the student affairs organization in particular. New professionals—those who often work most closely with students—are key to engaging students in the programs and services that lead to achievement of those goals.

Authenticity

As noted above, data collected through a sound assessment process contribute to the robust body of evidence necessary for an organization to grow and improve practice. To gain a better understanding of the impact of services, student affairs organizations should develop strong learning outcomes and conduct assessment to measure progress in achievement of those outcomes. The data gathered from outcomes-based assessment inform practice and demonstrate the impact of programs and services for the students we serve.

Walvoord (2004) highlighted three commonly accepted steps to assessment: identify the outcome, gather evidence, and use information for improvement. The evidence gathered from assessment leads to greater transparency and data-informed decision making, which are key tenets of authenticity. The data from effective assessment plans can be used to support institutional scorecards, institution-wide strategic indicators, and factbook information that features students' cocurricular activities. Data must be collected authentically, or with rigor, to have an impact on improving practice. All research, including action research designed to inform practice, should follow basic protocols, including relevant guidelines for data collection (quantitative, qualitative, or mixed method, which are featured in other sections of this volume). Poor data collection leads to misinterpretations. This, in turn, can lead to misinformed decisions, which can then lead to misguided changes to practice. Ultimately, poorly collected data hurt the authenticity of the assessment effort.

Assessment professionals have an obligation to ensure sound practices that guide each project and the overall assessment effort. Transparency at all levels of the assessment process—from design, to method, to reporting results in an unbiased and objective manner—is key to the authenticity of the assessment process. Transparency is the responsibility of each assessment professional.

Sustaining a Culture of Evidence

All student affairs organizations must develop a culture of evidence to support the decision-making processes of the division and the institution. The three overarching goals of any assessment culture are to focus on data-informed decision making, promote continuous improvement, and demonstrate how the division contributes to student learning. According to the American Association for Higher Education (2000), assessment is "most effective when it reflects an understanding of learning as multidimensional, integrated, and revealed in performance over time" (p. 2).

We must seek to understand culture in the larger context of higher education and explore relevant ramifications for student affairs professionals. Some scholars view culture as the beliefs, values, or assumptions shared by all members of an organization (Schein, 1992). This approach, which Martin (1992) terms the "integration perspective," assumes that values are apparent, are "shared by all members of a culture, in an organization-wide consensus" (p. 45), and that members clearly understand their roles in the culture. Studies organized around the integration perspective often have the expressed goal of utilizing culture to manage behaviors and beliefs, and only acknowledge the existence of conflict and subcultures at surface levels. Student affairs organizations follow a similar pattern when it comes to organizational culture. We believe that the 4 Cs of commitment, consistency, communication, and connection (Adams-Gaston & Kennedy-Phillips, 2015; Gansemer-Topf & Kennedy-Phillips, 2017) are components specifically valued in student affairs cultures. Realization of the 4 Cs requires the efforts of individual professionals at every level of the student affairs organization and the collective commitment of programs, units, and divisions.

Key Components: The 4 Cs

There are four components necessary to sustain a culture of evidence in any student affairs organization (Adams-Gaston & Kennedy-Phillips, 2015). "First, there must be *commitment* at all levels of the organization to assessment and data collection. Second, the organization must be *consistent* in all aspects of its assessment processes. Third, a strong culture of evidence maintains is *connected* to goals and outcomes internally and externally to the division. Finally, *communication* is key to developing a positive and sustained culture of evidence" (Gansemer-Topf & Kennedy-Phillips, 2017, p. 339).

Commitment

For a culture of evidence to be sustained, it needs executive support as well as ownership from all levels of the organization. In student affairs, we cannot have a culture of assessment without commitment from the chief student affairs officer (CSAO), who, as the leader, sets the overarching tone. Executive mandates flow throughout the division at all levels, which helps all staff—and new professionals in particular—understand the value of the assessment effort and see how their work supports institutional and divisional goals.

According to Kotter and Cohen (2002), "[assessment] initiatives flounder because they're headed up by people who lack the time or the clout to accomplish what is necessary" (p. 87). The assessment professional who oversees assessment should have an elevated position within the student affairs division and have the emotional intelligence and skills required to navigate the political environment to advance the assessment process.

CSAOs must devote adequate fiscal and personnel resources to assessment for it to be successful. Employing a dedicated assessment professional is ideal. However, some student affairs organizations do not have the resources to do so; in those cases, it is essential to provide support for staff to engage in assessment as part of their work responsibilities.

Building staff capacity is a key foundation of an assessment and data collection process; assessment that is not grounded in good practice by trained staff will fail. Professional development and training opportunities related to assessment and data collection are sponsored in many areas of the country and online. NASPA and ACPA host conferences and webinar series specifically designed to build assessment capacity in student affairs. Other organizations, such as the Association for Institutional Research (AIR), are growing their resources in this arena. Staff members should also seek out institution-sponsored opportunities for skill development.

Personal commitment to assessment is important. The acquisition and continued development of assessment-related knowledge and skills contributes to one's career value. In addition to individual development, professional growth in these areas adds value to the student affairs division and the institution. We believe that *all* professionals have an obligation to use evidence to demonstrate the value of our work, regardless of our roles and responsibilities.

Consistency

Assessment must be part of student affairs' normal operations; it is more than an initiative. When done with consistency, assessment adds value to an organization's ability to be innovative and to adapt to changes in the student body specifically, and within the institutional overall. An effective assessment process is consistent, fits the unique needs of the student affairs division, and provides a documented process for the collection and analysis of evidence to demonstrate the efficacy of programs and services.

It is important to assess the assessment process, but for it to remain useful the process must not experience significant changes from year to year. Consistency helps to sustain reliable data over time and it also encourages staff to stay engaged in the process. A consistent and reliable assessment plan and evidence collection process yield strong trend data for the organization; in turn, this bolsters a culture of evidence and informs the development of new programs and services. Furthermore, it supports clear communication, including a strong narrative for the student affairs division regarding the impact of its work on the achievement of institutional goals.

All professionals learn from and value a steady, dependable process, which is particularly helpful for new staff. In each role a professional assumes, it takes time to learn about and understand consistency in that specific setting. When new to a position, one has an opportunity to observe and ask questions to garner a contextualized understanding of assessment and data-informed decision making. Intentional efforts to learn, and to share that knowledge with others, help establish an atmosphere of collaboration in which consistency is achieved through the collective commitment to cultures of evidence.

Connection

Assessment processes and data collection efforts must be connected to the larger goals of the institution. This helps staff see how their work in particular, and the work of student affairs overall, contributes to student learning and success. It also highlights a key aspect of higher education: learning takes place at all levels of the college or university. As Pelletier, Oaks, and Kennedy-Phillips (2013) described, "the most specific [are] the program- or activity-level outcomes, and the broadest/most general [are] the division-level outcomes" (p. 22). Maki

(2004) explained, "there is an underlying coherence [between levels of outcomes] that contributes to student learning" (p. 62).

A connected process enhances our ability to collaborate with colleagues across the institution. Student learning does not take place in silos. Furthermore, students see the college or university through the prism of their needs and goals, and a siloed approach to any function in academia—including assessment—fails to honor their holistic experiences. A culture of evidence relies on collaboration across the institution and requires clear communication of the assessment process and expected outcomes.

Communication

As Gansemer-Topf and Kennedy-Phillips (2017) noted, "without transparent, clear, and frequent communication, a sustained, strong culture of evidence is not possible" (p. 340). The communication of assessment results will give the student affairs division an opportunity to lead with its narrative. Evidence should be communicated regularly with all members of the institutional community, including faculty, staff, administrators, students, friends of the student affairs division, and key stakeholders. Clear and consistent articulation builds confidence in the work at all levels; it also recognizes an expanded definition of decision makers (Swing & Ross, 2016b).

In particular, sharing assessment results with students fosters their interest in the work and encourages their further involvement in data collection activities. Faculty members appreciate evidence that highlights connections between the curricular and the cocurricular. Friends of the division and key stakeholders, such as alumni and prospective donors, value knowing how their engagement with the division leads to outcomes. And all stakeholders, including administrators at all levels of the institution, use assessment information to make decisions.

All higher education professionals, regardless of roles and responsibilities, must maintain transparent, clear, and frequent communication in support of a strong culture of evidence. Communication—verbal, and interpersonal—is the responsibility of every professional at every level of the institution. Each of us can invest in our skills through training opportunities, formal and informal mentoring, and collaboration with colleagues. Ideas range from inviting other professionals to proof our written work, practicing presentations to ensure that we articulate key points (regardless of whether we plan to share information at a staff meeting, present results to another department, or deliver a conference session), and exploring best practices. At the base level, we must know our audiences, refrain from inundating people with extraneous information, and remember that the onus is on us to ensure that others understand the information we communicate.

A key communication-related opportunity when establishing a culture of evidence is to showcase best practices within the student affairs organization. Doing so celebrates positive activities, conveys the division's values, and communicates progress towards fulfilling the institution's mission and goals.

Politics: Context and Nuance

As noted throughout this chapter, context matters—not only in creating and sustaining a culture of evidence, and in maintaining ethical standards, but also in navigating the political landscape of higher education. It seems that any work designed to improve institutions in support of student success would be altruistic in nature and free of political nuance. Yet institutions are intricate networks of responsibility, authority, and resources, and they are held accountable to their missions by a wide array of stakeholders. As such, information is a valuable asset, and as a producer and consumer of information, the field of assessment is a key player in the political arena.

Assessment happens across the institution—formally and informally—regardless of whether all of it is officially recognized or coordinated. In higher education, we tend to dismiss "unauthorized" uses of data and information in deference to "one source of the truth." Yet that "one source of the truth is quickly being replaced with data inspection through many lenses, creating an array of varying conclusions derived from the same raw data" (Swing & Ross, 2016a). When we ignore work outside of our purview simply because it is not "ours," silos develop, inefficiencies abound, and opportunities to develop common understandings and protocols while sharing the workload burden are lost. Although individual assessment initiatives are designed to explore specific questions, greater gains are realized when all stakeholders are considered and data capacity in all units is recognized. The need for control often results in fear of messiness and the tendency for turf wars, but with collaboration, efficiencies are realized and a more robust culture of evidence develops (Ross & Lewis, 2017).

To fully understand the political context of assessment, it is helpful to consider whom assessment serves. Swing and Ross (2016b) reminded us that in addition to senior leaders, a wide range of decision makers "impact an institution's achievement of its mission," including "students shaping their own experiences, faculty shaping their teaching and interactions with students, and staff shaping program designs and direct interactions with students" (p. 1). If assessment solely or primarily supports senior decision makers, or if the products of assessment are consumed in silos without regard for the larger institutional context, a culture of evidence is not sustained.

Recognition of decision makers across the institution (and when relevant, beyond the institution) as consumers is required if a culture of evidence is to be achieved. However, the reality is that demands for information are ever increasing, all decision makers are important, and attempts to prioritize their needs are laden with political nuance. As higher education professionals, our priorities are determined by the goals set forth for our institutions, divisions, units, and programs. We must navigate the political landscape within our own spheres of influence to help our work achieve its full potential value.

As stated at the beginning of this chapter, we believe that it is of utmost importance for each of us to learn as much as we can about our institutions overall, and develop understandings of the various political contexts at play. To do so, we must build networks with colleagues in other units and divisions, learn where pockets of expertise exist, and identify opportunities to collaborate. It is only then that our work can transcend the limitations of political agendas in service of the greater good; that is, so that assessment can achieve its optimal value as relevant, intentional, sustainable, and authentic. The products of assessment have limited value and reach if we do not pay attention to how the process of assessment fits within a culture of evidence, acknowledge an expanded set of decision makers (consumers), and utilize capacity throughout the institution (producers).

Context matters. Knowing our audiences matters. Understanding our institutions' cultures matters. Establishing collegial relationships across our institutions provides opportunity to navigate this political space in support of robust cultures of evidence.

Case Study

The Second-year Transformational Experience Program (STEP) at The Ohio State University is an example of how assessment data are used to drive decisions at the highest levels of an organization. The program is focused on student success and is led by the student affairs division. It provides a case study for the ethical use of university data and the politics that surround a $300-million capital investment. Following is a description of the program.

Ohio State's Second-year Transformational Experience Program (STEP) was developed as a continuation of the university's effort to redefine the student experience. Before STEP was implemented, The Ohio State University commissioned a study to identify the predictors of second-year student success and they were found to be:

- Participation in campus events.
- Living on campus.
- Peer interaction.
- Interaction with faculty.
- Institutional commitment.

Another survey showed that students who live on campus participate in campus activities much more (82%) than those who live off-campus (64%). Data also indicated that students who live on-campus for two years have higher graduation and two-year retention rates than students who did not live on campus their first two years:

- Graduation Rate: 88.2% compared to 76.5% (2005 cohort).
- Retention Rate: 95.7% compared to 88.6% (2009 cohort).

This 2012/2013 survey (entitled HOME), given to all students who lived in Ohio State residence halls, showed that 84% of those students credit their housing situation with their connectedness to the university.

STEP is designed to focus on student success and development and to enable students to engage in activities that cater to their individual interests and needs. Through interaction with faculty, students are able to develop tools for life and build essential network connections. By fulfilling the program requirements, students are eligible to receive a fellowship of up to $2,000 to use towards a STEP Signature

Project they might otherwise not be able to do (Source: 2017 The Ohio State University–STEP: Second-Year Transformational Experience Program step.osu.edu).

Given the level of investment the university has made in STEP, significant evidence is needed to move this program forward. Imagine you are one of the student affairs professionals leading this effort. How would you answer the following questions?

1. What ethical considerations do you need to be aware of when championing this program?
2. How would you apply the 4 Cs of sustaining a culture of evidence (commitment, consistency, connection, communication)?
3. How would a lack of transparency impact successful adoption of STEP?
4. Describe the politics of implementing a program of this scope. Keep in mind the concepts shared in The Student Affairs Reality and Politics: Context and Nuance sections of this chapter.

Chapter Assessments

Teacher's Assessment of Student
The student should be able to:
1. Connect the concepts of data and information literacy, data quality, and data use within the context of STEP.
2. Identify the roles of transparency and political nuance within the context of STEP. Discussion can be guided by the ideas of competition for scarce resources and the role of student affairs in supporting learning and in resource stewardship.
3. Describe the necessity of collaboration and attention to the needs of myriad stakeholders within the context of STEP.
4. Articulate why a culture of evidence is key to fulfilling the goals of STEP.

Student Self-assessment

1. Of the concepts shared in this chapter, which are new to you and which are more familiar to you?

2. What experiences would be helpful to you in expanding your familiarity with the concepts shared in this chapter? Opportunities may include informational interviews and conversations with higher education professionals across the institution, job shadowing, expanded duties and responsibilities, and professional development or skill-based training. Describe specific action steps you plan to take to grow your knowledge.

Chapter 4

ASSESSMENT, EVALUATION,
AND RESEARCH (AER) DESIGN

Jen Wells and Martha Glass

Understanding the Need for Assessment

As noted in Chapters 1 and 2, assessment has been long recognized as a best practice for the student affairs profession. Conducting assessment and then using data for informed decision making are keys to increasing the accountability of programs and services emanating from student affairs and the "professionalization" of this discipline. Data also assists in more effectively "telling our story" (Bingham, Bureau, & Duncan, 2015; Henning & Roberts, 2016; Yousey-Elsener, Bentrim, & Henning, 2015). However, to be more effective, student affairs educators would benefit from additional training to enhance their knowledge, understanding, and application in assessing learning and student success and evaluating programs (Bresciani, Moore Gardner, & Hickmott, 2009; Henning & Roberts, 2016; Sandeen & Barr, 2006; Schuh & Associates, 2009).

Assessment in student affairs is essential to improve programs and services, to identify strengths as well as growth opportunities, and to evaluate whether or not the needs of the student population are being met. As noted in earlier chapters, there is an increased demand for accountability and quality in higher education and student affairs is certainly not immune to this call. There are both external and internal stakeholders to higher education institutions that expect student affairs professionals to engage in assessment practice. Institutions are accountable to students, families, local communities, alumni, faculty, public and private funders, and policy makers. They are also accountable to the student affairs profession, broadly (e.g., ACPA/NASPA, CAS), and to the many functional area professional associations such as but not limited to the National Academic Advising Association (NACADA), Association of College and University Housing Officers–International (ACUHO-I), and Career Services (NACE).

There are internal and external pressures, along with the need for success metrics that drive assessment practice. However, the main purposes of assessment are to answer important questions about student learning and development and to use the answers to shape quality educational programing. Many of the questions asked include:

- What is the purpose of the unit?
- What outcomes are important and relevant?
- What will the program/event/initiative accomplish?
- What do students need to be successful?
- What is our role in the success of students?
- What will students need to be able to do and/or know as a result of the course/workshop/orientation/program?
- What is the evidence that student learning and/or development is occurring?
- How do we know students are learning what we expect them to learn?
- How is the information used that is collected?
- Where is there room for improvement?

When we engage in assessment and think about our work in a different way, we move from planning activities and *doing* things to thinking about how to impact student success, improve programs and services, and ensure quality student engagement in the process. The question changes from "What are we going to do?" to "How will students develop, change, and grow as a result of what we do?" or "Are we meeting students' needs in order to provide an environment conducive for learning and development to occur?"

As noted earlier, the ACPA and NASPA Professional Competency Rubric (2016) defined assessment design as

> Know theoretical frameworks that align with organizational outcomes, goals, and values. Ability to create learner-centered out-

comes that align with divisional and institutional priorities; to design and lead a process-oriented strategy to address the assessment's purpose or research questions. Develop disposition to think critically and systematically about questions and problems of practice. (pg. 14)

The assessment, evaluation, and research (AER) design rubric includes three competency (skill) levels: foundational, intermediate, and advanced (Table 4.1); the themes underlying these levels are outcomes, processes and strategy, and disposition. The next three sections of this chapter are based on the aforementioned areas (purpose, strategy, and disposition) and will be described based on the three competency levels.

Table 4.1
ACPA & NASPA PROFESSIONAL COMPETENCY RUBRIC (2016) FOR AER DESIGN

Foundational	Intermediate	Advanced
• Design program and learning outcomes that are clear, specific, and measurable; informed by theoretical frameworks and aligned with organizational outcomes, goals, and values. • Utilize theoretical frameworks and organizational outcomes, goals, and values to design program and learning outcomes. • Explain to students and colleagues the relationship of AER processes to learning outcomes and goals. values.	• Prioritize program and learning outcomes with organization's goals and values. • Utilize student learning and development theories and scholarly research to inform ontent and design of learning outcomes and assessment tools. • Educate stakeholders about the relationship of departmental AER processes to learning outcomes and goals at the student, department, division, and institutional level. • Discern appropriate design(s) based on critical questions, available data, and intended audience(s).	• Lead the conceptualization and design of ongoing, systematic, high-quality, data-based strategies at the institutional, divisional, and/or unit-wide level to evaluate and assess learning, programs, services, and personnel. • Use assessment and evaluation results in determining institutional, divisional, or unit accomplishments toward mission/goals, re-allocation of resources, and advocacy for more resources. • Lead a comprehensive communication process to inform campus stakeholders about the relationship of AER processes to learning outcomes, and goals at the student, department, division, and institution level.

Often, when we talk about assessment, there is a desire to move quickly to gathering evidence; however, assessment begins prior to data collection. There must be a systematic and ongoing plan for assessment and the collection of information (Henning & Roberts, 2016). Before student affairs educators begin to collect data or make decisions about programs and services, they must first be clear about the expected outcomes.

Defining Outcomes

Outcomes are foundational to AER work and reinforce the creation of intentional learning experiences and environments for students to succeed, learn, and gain skills aligned with the purpose of the unit, program, or workshop. Prior to writing outcomes, though, one must know and understand the mission and goals of the department, division and the institution. If you are designing a new program, you may need to create these statements before outcomes are developed. Below we outline each of these important AER terms and explain how they should align.

> **Mission statement** describes the broad shared purpose and vision of the organization. A college or university will have mission statements at multiple levels; alignment across the levels of shared purpose is extremely important. Department mission statements will also need to align with these statements.
>
> **Goals** are comprehensive statements that reflect the broad, overarching, long-range intentions of the division or department (Bresciani et al., 2009). At the department level, goals reflect the core functions. Goals will generally reflect the key terms in the mission statement, the *why* for the department, the big things that the department, unit, or program accomplishes with its work. Goals alone are broad statements that will need to be broken down into statements that can be measured.
>
> **Outcomes** are specific statements about how the student or program will be different as a result of programming. They determine the impact services, programs, and environments have on students' learning, development, and success. And as such, they should align with an organization's mission statement and goals.

Generally, goals do not change on an annual basis, as they provide the general direction for an institution's, division's, or department's purpose or strategic initiatives. Across these levels, though, goals are aligned by shared purpose. Goals are then broken down into measurable units called outcomes. Outcomes are what are assessed, with that assessment providing evidence of meeting the intended purposes of educational experiences and environments. According to Henning and Roberts (2016), "outcomes help determine what should be assessed, guide planning, direction in developing strategies for achievement, and communicate to stakeholders what they are doing and the impact they are having" (p. 87).

At the foundational level, you will want to ensure that students and colleagues understand the relationship between goals and outcomes. As you advance to the intermediate stage, it will be important to stakeholders that the goals and outcomes of the department relate to the division's and university's strategic directions. At the advanced level, it is important to have a full, comprehensive communication plan to address these relationships. Perhaps this would include visuals or dashboards to show progress on goals; a transparent action plan with metrics for each goal; and/or a graphical representation of the relationship between the goals, outcomes, and processes for evaluation.

Understanding Outcome Development

Once you have gained an understanding of how the mission and the goals all relate, the next component in developing the outcomes are the theories that will be used to form the outcomes. Before developing or identifying outcomes, think about theories that influence their development as well as the environment and culture of the unit, division, and institution. Theoretical frameworks that shape outcomes in student affairs include psychosocial and identity development, cognitive-structural, typology, and person-environment. Insights on the goals and outcomes of the environment and culture of the unit, division, and institution can be identified by reviewing important documents such as mission statements, strategic plans, recent program reviews, action plans, identified goals, and previous assessment findings. New professionals should review department mission and values statements, strategic plans, and identified goals. Department leaders should think about the division mission and strategic direction of the unit as it aligns with the university. Senior-level positions with leadership in divisional assessment will want to provide the mission, goals, and strategic priorities to all departments. It is important to be clear about the expectations of leaders in the division, the institution's mission, and how priorities sometimes change or evolve.

As noted, alignment across institutional levels is an important part of outcome development. Considering these factors will allow you to show how your department, programs, and services advance the mission of the university. When your assessment efforts align with these factors, it is another form of accountability. In addition, when efforts across departments are in alignment, this creates a more robust learning environment for students. For example, students engaged in recreation sports programs to build leadership skills, and student volunteer programs also geared to building leadership skills, can provide multiple touch points toward the same goals.

Developing a Framework for Writing Outcomes

There are two primary categories of outcomes: learning and development outcomes and program and operational outcomes. Learning and development outcomes are statements that explain the shifts in knowledge, skills, attitudes, and dispositions expected of students who engage in student affairs programs and services. Program and operational outcomes are usually related to more administrative functions like process improvement, resource management, satisfaction, participation rates, and utilization of services (Henning & Roberts, 2016). Both types of outcomes must be clear, specific, and measurable, as we will explore later in more detail. As a side note, don't let terminology stand in the way of good assessment practice. For example, in many assessment texts, the word objective is used interchangeably with outcome, but in some, they are defined a bit differently. For the purposes of this chapter, outcome is used to represent both.

As noted earlier, well-thought-out outcomes, especially learning outcomes, are grounded in theoretical frameworks. Student learning and development theories and scholarly research should inform outcome development. For example, career services may want to review literature on internships as high-impact practices; student leadership programs may want to review literature on servant-leadership; and diversity and inclusion programs may want to review literature on identity development. Using theory to develop outcomes and design programs is a cornerstone of the intermediate level of AER design. It is important to note that many theoretical frameworks will provide big, ideal outcomes that define comprehensive student development over time. When writing outcomes for a one-time program, be realistic about the expected impact that will occur in that specific program. As Wise and Barham (2012) noted:

> When deciding what programs and services to measure, select those that address program goals, those related to longer interventions. Typically, the longer the intervention the greater the likelihood of achieving the outcomes for which we hoped. For example, if an outcome is to increase student leadership skills, then a program that lasts one day versus two hours has a greater likelihood of increasing student leadership skills. (p. 29)

A helpful tool in developing learning outcomes is the latest version of Bloom's Taxonomy (2001), as it provides a framework for understanding the differences in types of learning at various levels. Bloom (1956) originally identified six categories for educational goals: knowledge, comprehension, application, analysis, synthesis, and evaluation. In 2001, a team of specialists in cognitive psychology, curriculum theory, instructional research, and testing and assessment revised the taxonomy (Anderson & Krathwohl, 2001). They identified six cognitive processes and used action verbs—remembering, understanding, applying, analyzing, evaluating, creating—rather than the nouns in the original taxonomy. The six processes of progressive learning move up levels of learning from knowledge to comprehension, application, analysis, and synthesis to evaluation. The taxonomy is often visualized as a pyramid with increasing cognitive complexity. There are a number of sample verbs associated with each process; they provide a helpful resource when writing learning and development outcomes. Based on the work of Anderson and Krathwohl (2001), Azusa Pacific University created a helpful table with sample verbs for each level (see Table 4.2).

In addition, several professional organizations have developed learning outcomes that are linked to student development theories. Among these are AAC&U's LEAP (2011), *Learning Reconsidered* (Keeling, 2004) and *Learning Reconsidered 2* (Keeling, 2006), and the *Degree Qualifications Profile* (DQP) (Adelman, Ewell, Gaston, & Schneider, 2011). The Council for the Advancement of Standards in Higher Education (CAS) (2015) promotes standards to enhance opportunities for student learning and development from higher education programs and services. The CAS student learning and development outcomes model is comprised of six broad categories (called

Table 4.2
MODIFIED VERSION OF BLOOM'S TAXONOMY ACTION VERBS

Definitions	I. Remembering	II. Understanding	III. Applying	IV. Analyzing	V. Evaluating	VI. Creating
Bloom's Definition	Exhibit memory of previously learned material by recalling facts, concepts, and answers.	Demonstrate understanding of facts and ideas by organizing, comparing, translating, interpreting, giving descriptions, and stating main ideas.	Solve problems to new situations by applying acquired knowledge, facts, techniques, and rules in a different way.	Examine and break information into parts by identifying motives or causes. Make inferences and find evidence to support generalizations.	Present and defend opinions by making judgments about information, validity of ideas, or quality of work based on a set of criteria.	Compile information together in a different way by combining elements in a new pattern or proposing alternative solutions.
Verbs	• Choose • Define • Find • How • Label • List • Match • Name • Omit • Recall • Relate • Select • Show • Spell • Tell • What • When • Where • Which • Who • Why	• Classify • Compare • Contrast • Demonstrate • Explain • Extend • Illustrate • Infer • Interpret • Outline • Relate • Rephrase • Show • Summarize • Translate	• Apply • Build • Choose • Construct • Develop • Experiment with • Identify • Interview • Make use of • Model • Organize • Plan • Select • Solve • Utilize	• Analyze • Assume • Categorize • Classify • Compare • Conclusion • Contrast • Discover • Dissect • Distinguish • Divide • Examine • Function • Inference • Inspect • List • Motive • Relationships • Simplify • Survey • Take part in	• Agree • Appraise • Assess • Award • Choose • Compare • Conclude • Criteria • Criticize • Decide • Deduct • Defend • Determine • Disprove • Estimate • Evaluate • Explain • Importance • Influence • Interpret • Judge	• Adapt • Build • Change • Choose • Combine • Compile • Compose • Construct • Create • Delete • Design • Develop • Discuss • Elaborate • Estimate • Formulate • Happen • Imagine • Improve • Invent • Make up

domains): knowledge acquisition, construction, integration and application; cognitive complexity; intrapersonal development; interpersonal competence; humanitarianism and civic engagement; and practical competence. Each domain includes dimensions, which further clarify the outcome areas and enable a more focused assessment approach based on institutional mission and priorities. If you elect to use learning outcomes developed by another organization, make sure that the outcomes align to the activities that will occur in the program so that they are relevant to the context.

Writing Clear Outcomes

After reviewing relevant theories tied to the student experience, you can now focus on developing specific student learning outcomes. While there are several models to use when developing outcomes, we use two models often in our own work: the SMART and ABCD models. The SMART approach for writing program or operational outcomes stands for specific, measurable, achievable/improvable, relevant, and time-bound:

Specific. The outcome wording is clear and unambiguous. Definite terms describe expected abilities, knowledge, values, attitudes, and performance. For example, wording an outcome *"to increase the number of students participating"* is more specific than stating *"to encourage participation."*

Measurable. This means clear criteria for measurement is defined so evidence can be provided related to progress on the outcome. Choosing the right verb will help determine whether the outcome can be measured using quantitative, qualitative, or mixed methods. For example, *"students will articulate three strengths"* is a measurable outcome.

Achievable. The outcome is realistic and has the potential to move the program or functional unit forward; it can be reasonably achieved; it is focused on an area of improvement; and the improvement on the outcome can be demonstrated.

Relevant. The outcome is related to the purpose, mission, and strategic priorities of the unit, department, division, and/or institution.

Time-bound. The outcome describes a specific time period for accomplishing the outcome. For example, *"students will apply to* *graduate school"* is not time-bound. A SMART outcome would read, *"students in the pre-law society will apply to at least one graduate school before commencement."*

Following are a few examples of SMART outcomes that focus on program and learning outcomes.

Program Outcomes

- Increase during the fall semester the number of students who include transferable skills on their resumes.
- Enhance professional development opportunities for Division employees during their first five years of employment.
- Increase by the end of the fall semester the percentage of students living on campus who complete the Gallup Strengths assessment.
- By the end of the academic year, the student health center will increase the percentage of students receiving nutrition counseling.

Learning Outcomes

- Students who participate in the six-week leadership seminar will be able to describe their leadership philosophy.
- Students will create and implement a project management plan in their first year of the Student Leadership Program.
- Students in the Service Learning Leadership Program will demonstrate increased leadership skills by the end of the semester by successfully completing a leadership skills inventory.

The ABCD model for writing learning and development outcomes has four aspects to address: audience, behavior, condition, and degree of achievement.

Audience. Who is the learner being addressed in the program? Make sure to identify if it is a specific group of students.

Behavior. What will the learner think, know, or do as a result of a program, service or intervention? What action will be demonstrated and then measured? This is where the verbs identified in the Bloom's taxonomy are used.

Condition. Identify the condition under which the desired behavior will occur. Will the behavior occur in a workshop, living-learning community, service-learning project, participation in student organization, a presentation, to name a few?
Degree of achievement. This is the minimum accepted performance expected for "participants" to demonstrate. How well or how much of behavior must be performed to be acceptable?

Example of the ABCD outcome with each item labeled.

By participating in the **Writing Outcomes workshop** (condition), **participants** (audience) will be able to **write one** (degree of achievement) **outcome statement** (behavior).

Here are a few examples of learning outcomes using the ABCD model:

- As a result of participating in Resident Assistant (RA) training, RAs will be able to assess the strengths and weaknesses of their leadership skills.
- As a result of participating in the International Peer Mentorship program, students will be able to identify three similarities and three differences they have with someone from a different background.
- As a result of completing Orientation Leader training, students will be able to identify at least one on-campus resource related to academics, health, relationships, career, finance, and alcohol.

There are also specific guidelines to address when writing quality outcomes

1. **Avoid the use of double-barreled outcomes**. Outcomes with the word "and" most likely need to be split into two outcome statements. In this example, *"students will demonstrate written, oral, and nonverbal communication skills"* means that students could address written and oral skills but not nonverbal skills so the outcomes, in part, would not be met.
2. **Write outcomes that measure changes in behavior or knowledge in terms that are observable**. For example, *"stu-*

dents will explain the steps to register for fraternity and sorority recruitment" measures knowledge as compared to *"students will feel confident about the steps in fraternity and sorority recruitment,"* which is an emotion.

3. **Choose quality outcomes over quantity**. Start small with manageable, measurable outcomes. It is better to focus on two or three well-written, measurable outcomes than to have more outcomes that are poorly constructed. If too many outcomes are included, it can be overwhelming and difficult to measure each and thus generate usable data.

Outcomes are similar to research questions as they define the direction and narrow the scope of the problem or question; an outcomes-based approach to assessment provides direction, alignment, and evidence to inform the work of student affairs professionals. As Bresciani, Moore Gardner, and Hickmott (2009) stated, "Outcomes-based assessment is designed as a systematic and critical process that yields information about what programs, services, or functions of a student affairs department or division positively contribute to students' learning and success, and which ones should be improved" (p. 16).

Self-assessment. As the Director of a Student Leadership Development program, you are interested in conducting an assessment of this program's impact on student learning and development.

1. Using the SMART model, write one program or operational outcome for your Student Leadership Development program.

2. Label the following outcome using the ABCD Model: *As a result of participating in the Leadership 101 workshop, student employees will explain three of the five leadership traits in Kouzes and Posner's (2017) The Leadership Challenge.*

3. Write two learning outcomes for your program using the ABCD Model, but this time apply a verb from two of the six levels of Bloom's Revised Taxonomy.

As you have gleaned by now, developing and writing outcomes is an important step in the assessment process, because outcomes are part of a larger assessment planning process.

Assessment Planning Process

"Plans are nothing, planning is everything" —Dwight D. Eisenhower

Eisenhower was not commenting on assessment planning, but we know from personal experience that having a well-planned assessment process is paramount to success. The assessment process begins with the end in mind; that is, the outcomes (impact) that are hoped for as a result of programming. The assessment process is often visualized as a cyclical model. A Google search will result in countless example images of assessment cycles adopted by institutions of higher education. We reviewed many of these as well as those cited in the literature. Across the examples, most contain four or five key elements that focus on (a) developing outcomes or goals, (b) implementing learning or development opportunities, (c) collecting and analyzing data, (d) reporting findings, and (e) using results for improvement. The four-step model shown in Figure 4.1 (Suskie, 2018, p. 9) offers a continuous approach to teaching, learning, and assessment.

1. Establish Learning Goals

4. Use the Results

2. Provide Learning Opportunities

3. Assess Student Learning

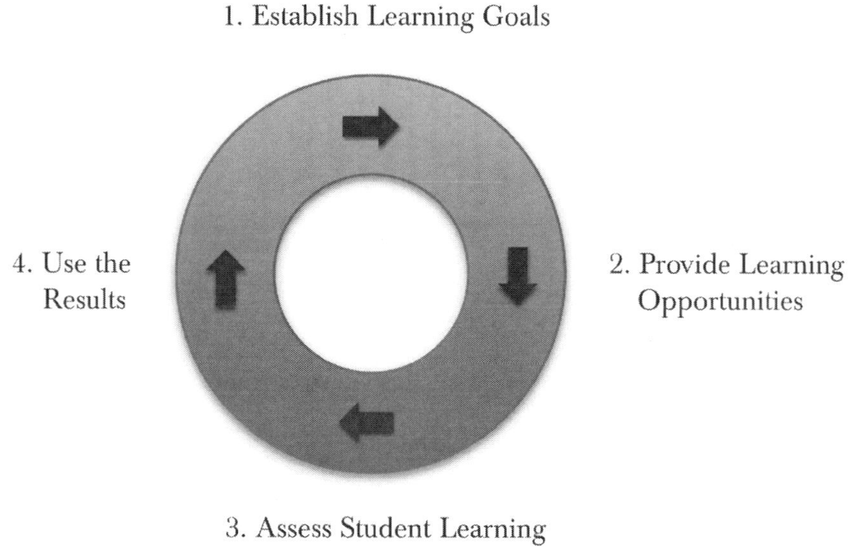

Figure 4.1. Teaching, Learning, and Assessment as a Continuous Four-Step Cycle.

The CAS Assessment Services Standards and Guidelines (2017) suggest that programs and services may want to include the following steps in their assessment cycle:

- Set program goals and learning and development outcomes.
- Develop and implement assessment strategies.
- Review and interpret findings.
- Develop a plan for data use and ongoing improvement.
- Implement plan and document evidence of ongoing improvement.

The National Institute for Learning Outcomes Assessment (NILOA) (2011) recommends transparency through the entire process to ensure that evidence of student accomplishments is accessible and readily available. There are six components, as shown in Figure 4.2 of the Transparency Framework.

Figure 4.2. NILOA Transparency Framework.

Many institutions adopt an assessment cycle, which is then reflected in their assessment planning and reporting templates. For example, all units at Kennesaw State University (n.d.), including student affairs, use an assessment plan and an improvement report. All programs, in their assessment plan, must identify the following:

Outcome: Identify an area of focus for improvement and alignment to the university strategic plan.
Measures: Identify the specific methods used to collect evidence, direct and/or indirect, of the outcome.
Data source: Identify the data source (institutional data; survey; rubric) and whether the data source is a direct or indirect form of evidence.

Beyond the assessment plan specified, all Kennesaw State programs must also complete an improvement report where they share (a) results in aggregated form for each measure; (b) improvement(s) that are warranted based on data and trends, including information from previous cycles on outcomes measured on more than one occasion; and (c) the strategies for improvement that will be implemented during the next assessment cycle.

We hope it is apparent that outcomes are the structural foundation of solid AER design. Outcomes, aligned with institutional goals and strategies, provide the stability for the structure to stand. Without a strong base, structures are vulnerable; similarly, outcomes provide the foundation for learning improvement and student success. Because we recognize and value the importance of student learning, we often only focus on these types of outcomes. We would like you to consider the step approach to outcomes and assessment planning as shown in Figure 4.3. Think of it this way—if we understand the needs of our students and ensure needs are being addressed, then we are also assured that environment is set up for learning to occur.

In the step approach, it is essential to understand the difference between needs, program evaluation, satisfaction, and learning assessment. Needs assessment is conducted to help answer the question, *What do students need in order to be successful?* "Assessing student needs is the process of determining the presence or absence of the factors and conditions, resources, services, and learning opportunities that students need in order to meet their educational goals and objectives

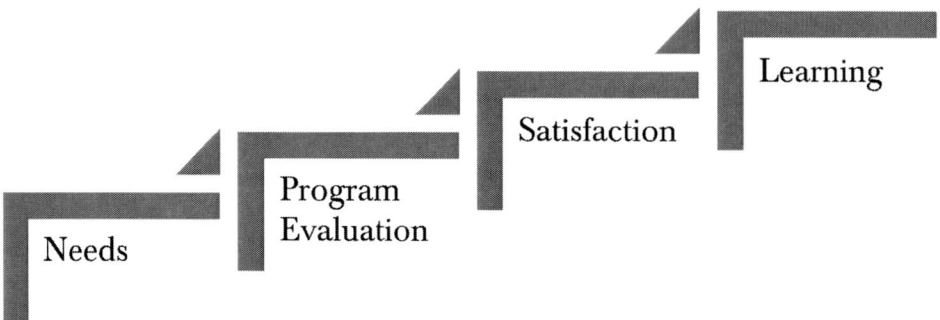

Figure 4.3. The Step Approach to Outcomes and Assessment Planning.

within the context of an institution's mission" (Upcraft & Schuh, 1996, p. 128). A needs assessment helps to make decisions about policies, programs, and services and can provide justifications for initiating, eliminating, or maintaining programs.

Program evaluation focuses on how well the program/activity/service met its intended purpose. It can also help answer questions about how well students' needs were met. Questions about the utilization of services, participation in programs, and student engagement can all be answered through program evaluation.

Satisfaction assessment focuses on the students' wants and levels of satisfaction. We would like to caution you not to focus only on this type of assessment. While it can feel good to know that students like what we offer, it is even more rewarding to know that our programs and services made an impact and that students learned. Satisfaction assessment is best used for areas that focus on customer service.

Learning assessment helps answer questions about what students are learning from the programs, services, and activities we provide. It is grounded in the outcomes-based approach. Institutions of higher education must determine what knowledge, skills, and dispositions students are gaining from both their curricular and cocurricular experiences.

Needs and satisfaction assessment are often confused. Students talk about their needs, but in reality, they are sometimes referencing what they want. Consider the following as an example of the difference. Your current laptop is large and heavy with a wide screen and a number pad. You travel a lot and find that is not easy to carry and you can't work while you are on the plane, as it won't fit on the tray.

You receive a Dell laptop that is small, lighter, and has all of the software you need when you travel, but you are disappointed because you wanted a MacBook. The Dell meets all your needs, but it's not what you wanted. As you explore and navigate the difference between a want and a need, remember the laptop analogy.

Strategic Assessment

In many cases, units find themselves with an abundance of assessment questions and outcomes. Similar to survey fatigue, there is also assessment fatigue. A combination of the step approach and alignment with the mission, goals, and strategic plans can be helpful in narrowing down the number of assessment questions and developing a comprehensive, practical plan going forward. We would always recommend that fewer outcomes assessed using the full cycle will be more meaningful than many outcomes that never leave the data collection phase.

Assessment mapping is another tool that can be used to prioritize and identify outcomes and assessment questions. Assessment mapping provides a visual representation of the alignment process. A mapping document shows how the learning, development, or program goals and outcomes link to the department or university programs and services. Maps can be created at a variety of levels and at different points in the assessment planning process. Mapping helps identify opportunities for learning, gaps and points of assessment, and makes learning transparent. Mapping helps to align strategies with outcomes and illustrates how the curriculum and cocurriculum are integrated to promote holistic learning and development. Mapping can also be used to identify opportunities for collaboration between departments. Suskie (2009) stated, "there is no point assessing something students don't have an opportunity to learn" (p. 99). Mapping is a great strategy to ensure students have the opportunities to learn the things we have identified as important. There are several different levels of maps (department/program, unit level, division level, and university level) as well as types (resources and outcomes). Resource maps are used to determine how inputs (invested resources) align with the activity, project, or workshops. They can also be used to see how resources are aligned with strategic goals or outcomes. According to Bresciani, Moore Gardner, and Hickmott (2009), "when an institution can identify which programs align intended outcomes with strategic or fund-

Table 4.3
AN EXAMPLE RESOURCE MAP

Inputs (resources that are invested)	Activity/Project/ Workshop 1	Activity/Project/ Workshop 2	Activity/Project/ Workshop 3	Activity/Project/ Workshop 4
Staff				
Time				
Dollars				
Technology				
Equipment				

ing priorities, the institution can tell more quickly how targeted funding is influencing expected improvements in the strategic areas identified" (p. 41). Table 4.3 provides one example of a map to identify resource use (Wise, 2014).

Outcome maps, in contrast, are designed to make explicit the activities and programs specifically designed for students to achieve the intended learning outcomes. This also helps to identify when outcomes are introduced, reinforced, emphasized, or evaluated. Using a mapping approach ensures that activities align to outcomes, that students have opportunities to learn what they are expected to learn and those activities are aligned with the intended results (Bresciani, Moore Gardner, & Hickmott, 2009). Table 4.4 provides an example of a template map that aligns outcomes to activities, projects, or workshops

Table 4.4
AN EXAMPLE OUTCOME PROJECT CONCEPT MAPPING CHART

	Activity/Project/ Workshop 1	Activity/Project/ Workshop 2	Activity/Project/ Workshop 3	Activity/Project/ Workshop 4
Outcome 1				
Outcome 2				
Outcome 3				

Table 4.5
EXAMPLE MAP FOR WOMEN'S RESOURCE CENTER
MENTOR/MENTEE PROGRAM

	Program Activities				
Goals	*Work with Learning Tutors*	*Career Services Workshop*	*Writing Workshops*	*Monthly Presentations*	*Organized Socials*
To encourage academic success	X	X	X		
To support developing workforce skills		X			
To promote community building					X
Increase communication skills		X	X	X	

(Bresciani, 2003), and Table 4.5 shows a completed example of a map for a women's resource center and which outlines expectations for mentors and mentees (Wise, 2014).

The next example (Table 4.6) illustrates part of a more advanced level map. It accomplishes several goals related to alignment. The Division of Student Affairs at Virginia Tech has five divisional learning outcomes called the Aspirations for Student Learning. The division has learning outcomes for each aspiration. The learning outcomes fall into one of three categories; Exploratory (introductory), Practice (intermediate), and Live (advance). Cranwell International Center staff created this map to identify their intended student learning outcomes, the alignment of those outcomes with the Aspirations for Student Learning, and to identify where the learning takes place and at what degree. For example, the outcome "students will demonstrate civility when confronted with world views that oppose their own" aligns with the aspiration "practice civility." This outcome is addressed in many of the programs they provide, including Global

Ambassadors Retreat and the Appalachian Overnight Retreat, among several others. It is labeled with an "E" for explore, or introductory. This means that these experiences will provide opportunities for students to be introduced and perhaps demonstrate civility at an introductory level. This map also identifies areas where data can be collected for evidence of meeting a learning outcome. A quick assessment at several of these events could provide multiple data points for evidence of meeting the learning outcome. Finally, this type of map identifies gaps where learning outcomes are not being addressed. This may be purposeful or could identify an opportunity.

When developing assessment maps, some key strategies to remember are (a) keep it simple by starting with a specific program or department, as you can expand the map as needed or as processes become

Table 4.6
PORTION OF AN ADVANCED LEVEL OUTCOMES MAP

Learning Outcomes	*Aspiration*	*Global Ambassadors Retreat*	*International Tailgate*	*Pie Day*	*Global Ambassador Training I*
Students will be able to articulate cultural self-awareness	Self-understanding & integrity	E & P			E
Students will demonstrate curiosity towards other cultures	Curiosity	E	E	E	E
Students will demonstrate civility when confronted with worldviews that oppose their own	Civility	E			
Students will articulate how their personal values and beliefs impact their leadership role(s)	Courageous Leadership; Self-Understanding & Integrity	E & P			

more complex; (b) specify the intended outcomes, if a learning map; (c) describe the program and activity where the intended outcome will be met; and (d) determine if the activities, workshops, and/or projects are useful and appropriate in achieving the stated outcome, and make sure to identify any gaps (Bresciani, 2003; Wise, 2014).

Process and strategy are key components of successful AER design. Using an assessment cycle, identifying the type of assessment questions, and mapping are all helpful approaches. Remember, "effective assessment focuses on what's most important" (Suskie, 2018, p. 26). It is worth taking the time at the front end to think critically and make intentional decisions about the planning process.

Discussion Questions

1. Why is mapping important and helpful? How can you implement this approach into your work?

2. What do you think Eisenhower meant in his quote, "plans are nothing, planning is everything?" How does this apply to assessment, graduate school, being a new professional?

Self-assessment

As the Director of a Student Leadership Development program, you are interested in conducting an assessment of this program's impact on student learning and development. In the previous activity, earlier in this chapter, you developed outcomes for your program.

1. Design an assessment map of the learning outcomes for the program.

2. Using Suskie's assessment cycle provided earlier in this chapter, you will create an assessment plan for the program. Make sure to include all four aspects of the cycle.

Disposition

Previous chapters of this book, and the exercises and examples in this chapter collectively support your professional development and identity, or what we refer to as dispositions. Disposition is the ability to think critically and systematically about questions and programs of practice. The American Association for Higher Education (1992) developed *Nine Principles of Good Practice for Assessing Student Learning;* the purpose of which was to advance assessment as a powerful tool for educational improvement. Furthermore, the aim was to help professionals hone their approaches to student learning to make a true difference for students (Hutchings, Ewell, & Banta, 2013). Many of these nine principles reiterate information provided in this chapter.

As a student affairs professional, your AER practice should be driven by educational values supported by the institution, division, and your program. Stakeholders both internal and external to the institution influence these values. The practice of engaging in quality assessment holds you personally accountable to stakeholders, particularly to the students for whom programs are designed and for whom we hope to make the greatest impact on learning and development. As a result, the expectations are for student affairs educators to develop the competencies and skills to align assessment practices and outcomes with larger organizational (divisional and institutional) priorities, goals, and outcomes to create a solid foundation for ongoing processes and the design of assessment. There are different types of assessment approaches and it is important to conceptualize, align, and understand the priorities of your work. What story do you want to tell your stakeholders; what questions do you need to answer to advocate for resources; and how do you demonstrate support of the learning mission of the institution? AER design is the foundation to answering these questions. With an outcomes-based approach, intentional processes and strategies, and a disposition to evidence-based, data-informed work, you will master and advance through AER design competency.

In closing, and to capture what we think is the essence of disposition, we offer you an authors' note that addresses the mindset, philosophy, and approach we believe is imperative for AER design:

> In our experience, we have found that the term assessment conjures feelings of fear, frustration, and other negative emotions. We have also observed the pride, excitement, and sense of achievement that

happens from a successful assessment experience. We often ask those with whom we work to trust the process, allow us to guide them through, and show them why we love what we do. So far, we have been able to hold true to this. Assessment should be meaningful and inform your work. Please do not forget this. We firmly and strongly believe that assessment can add value, direction, and quality to your work. We have outlined in this chapter how to write outcomes and plan for a successful process. Without assessment you will not be able effectively do your job, answer the important questions around transparency, accountability, and return on investment, but we hope that as you explore and understand assessment, you will experience the value. We have countless stories and examples of success and believe that you all have the capacity to add to the continuous improvement narrative. A successful assessment project does not always mean positive results; it's like science, sometimes things do not work the way you may have hoped, but that is what leads to discovery. We have the opportunity through assessment to explore and make meaning of data to help guide us in the direction of improving the quality of experiences for our students. Assessment efforts are one tool to help you improve these experiences and tell your success stories. Please do not stop with the plan. Ask questions, execute a plan, explore the data, investigate strategies for improvement, and discover how the story of your work unfolds.

As you move forward in this book you will delve deeper into research design and acquire tools to identify key aspects of methodology, data collection, and data analysis to use in examining a current project or in building a new assessment, evaluation, or research (AER) project. The foundation provided in this chapter has prepared you for that next step.

Chapter 5

METHODOLOGY, DATA COLLECTION, AND DATA ANALYSIS

Ross E. Markle and Javarro A. Russell

In this chapter, we provide you with the tools to identify key aspects of *methodology, data collection,* and *data analysis,* which can be used to examine a current project or build a new assessment, evaluation, or research (AER) project. While this chapter does not offer an exhaustive review of statistics, research methods, and measurement, it provides simple strategies and considerations to foster your engagement with methods, measurement, and data. Terminology in this chapter is often defined through example, but if needed, please refer to Chapter 2 for further clarification of unfamiliar terms. Understanding through example is a good place to begin our exploration of *methodology, data collection,* and *data analysis* together.

Let's say that you want to assess the efficacy of a study abroad program to promote students' *willingness to engage in culturally diverse situations.* A senior administrator at your institution might agree that this is a reasonable and important project that could help demonstrate the effectiveness of the program and possibly guide future improvements. However, the ultimate quality and/or usefulness of examining the program will be determined by how the outcome is measured, from whom information is gathered, and how results are examined and interpreted.

Example 1: Upon returning from study abroad, students complete a survey that includes several questions about their interest in engaging in culturally diverse situations. These results are then compared to a similar survey sent to students who did not participate in study abroad.

Example 2: Prior to participating in study abroad, students write an essay about their previous experiences in culturally diverse situations. After study abroad, students are again asked to write about how they engaged in such settings, as well as what they have learned during their study abroad experience.

Both of these cases represent reasonable approaches to assessing students' willingness to engage in culturally diverse situations. However, both have their strengths and challenges—some inherent to their approach, others that could emerge upon implementation.

Comparisons between Assessment, Evaluation, and Research

As noted in Chapter 2, there are clear distinctions and similarities between assessment, evaluation, and research. The distinctions, in particular, have notable implications when it comes to identifying the methodology, data sources, and analyses you will use. In general, the higher the stakes in decision making that result from an AER process, the more thorough and extensive the methodology must be. Here, we define those consequences using three underlying themes that should be considered from the start when selecting the appropriate method, data collection, and analysis; these are the *stakes, scope,* and *audience* of the project.

Stakes refer to the intended use of a project's results, which vary across AER contexts. Let us return to the study abroad example. If you direct the study abroad program, it is quite possible that you might use assessment results only to obtain feedback to guide program improvements. However, if your goal is to obtain external funding, then it might be more advantageous to gather data through program evaluation. Program evaluation is often used to determine the worth or value of a program and involves using assessment evidence in decision making. On the other hand, if your goal is to develop a hypothesis about study abroad experiences and their impact on students' *engagement in culturally diverse situations,* you might decide to collect data by participating in a national research study on the effectiveness of study abroad programs. Compare both assessment (for improvement) and evaluation for (decision making) to research, and you will see that the consequences for use of data (and in decision making) increase with each.

The *scope* refers to the context in which results are likely to be used and the degree to which results will be generalized outside the program of study. Example 2 from the study abroad scenario is a reasonable way to assess student learning and development within the program. However, what if an institution wanted to evaluate how to best distribute resources among various cocurricular programs? The previous assessment results support the study abroad program, but they do little to show how similar learning might occur through other cocurricular programming. Moreover, findings from neither example are likely to generalize outside the program/university context.

Another consideration when selecting the appropriate method, data collection, and analysis is *audience*. The distinctions between assessment, evaluation, and research are based on use, and accordingly each intended use has a target audience. The audience for assessment is most often "internal" (e.g., program staff, immediate supervisor); evaluation may include a mixture of both internal and "external" audiences (e.g., senior administration, funding organizations); and research is almost wholly focused on external audiences (e.g., other researchers, professionals in the same field). For internal audiences, overly complex analyses might leave an audience either confused or unconvinced of the findings. For external audiences, if you choose a methodology that is overly simplistic and unconvincing, you may fail to demonstrate the level of evidence necessary in evaluative or research settings.

Throughout the rest of this chapter, we address some of the issues that may have been glossed over to this point—factors such as the number of students to be included in a study, representing various student groups, and selecting research methodologies. As you continue, keep in mind the issues of stakes, scope, and audience, and how they apply to the work you observe (from your peers, colleagues, or the literature you read) and perhaps even to your own AER, at present or in the future.

> **Self-assessment**
>
> **Understanding Consequences:** Think of an assessment, or evaluation, or research project with which you are familiar. How would you describe the stakes, scope, and audience of this project? Overall, how do these three combine to establish the consequences for use of data (and in decision making) with your project?
>
> **Setting the Context:** Use the same example as you progress through this chapter, as it will be helpful to apply these concepts in practice—even hypothetical practice. Write this example down and use it as you work through the self-assessment questions posed throughout this chapter.

Methodology

Distinctions between Qualitative and Quantitative

Regardless of whether you are conducting assessment, evaluation, or research, nearly all approaches for gathering information can be classified as quantitative or qualitative, or a combination of the two (mixed methods). The most common practical distinction between these methods is the type of information collected. Quantitative studies employ more traditional concepts of data (i.e., numbers) and statistics—counts of behavior, characteristics, or other phenomenon—that can be compared and analyzed in a variety of ways. The summarizing nature of quantitative data enables observation of large numbers of students, settings, and/or contexts. Qualitative studies typically use open-ended sources of data, such as interviews, essays, or observations, which allow richer and deeper understandings of the topic at hand. Mixed methods are procedures for collecting both qualitative and quantitative data in a single study. Mixing both quantitative and qualitative research and data enables greater breadth and depth of understanding.

The decision to use quantitative or qualitative inquiry and methodology is, in part, based on one's philosophical stance, or how one makes sense of the world. As Creswell (2014) has noted:

I see worldviews as a general philosophical orientation about the world and the nature of research that a researcher brings to a study. Worldviews arise based on discipline orientations, students' advisors/mentors inclinations, and past research experiences. The types of beliefs held by individual researchers based on these factors will often lead to embracing a qualitative, quantitative, or mixed methods approach in their research. (p. 6)

Beyond stance, personal preferences might also arise because of the practical implications of each method. For example, those who prefer the voice of the student—either through interviews, essays, or other forms of evidence that allow rich, individual responses—tend to prefer qualitative approaches. These tend to involve smaller samples of students. Conversely, those who wish to represent a large number of students, populations, and subpopulations, and even disaggregation of data by specified characteristics are more likely to employ quantitative methods.

Quantitative and qualitative approaches each differ by several other interrelated elements, including types of research questions, data collection approaches, data sources, data analysis methods, and reliability and validity (which are discussed later in this chapter). Why are these considered interrelated? Your choice of research question guides your study design and methodology (i.e., quantitative or qualitative methodology), which in turn guides data collection and analysis. Even discussions of reliability and validity change substantially (as does the terminology) when one elects to follow either a quantitative or a qualitative path.

Self-assessment—Choosing your Research Approach: Would you choose a quantitative or qualitative approach given your AER project? How is your decision influenced by (a) your personal preferences, (b) the context and consequences of the program, and (c) the practical limitations of accessing students, available data, etc.? (NOTE: After learning more about quantitative and qualitative methods, you may want to return and revisit your answer.)

Establishing "Research Questions"

Research questions can often be gleaned from the initial goals of an assessment, evaluation, or research project and what one intends to accomplish and learn in the process. It is our experience that well-established goals, created using a research-based mindset and process, provide a helpful guide to making decisions about method, data, and analyses. Wording of your research question(s) determines if you are interested in descriptive, relational, or causal relationships (quantitative study) or in exploring a phenomenon (qualitative study).

While there are many ways to compare and contrast research questions, we present two paradigms in Table 5.1 to guide the development of research questions in both quantitative and qualitative settings. There are two additional, important points to make regarding research questions. First, because qualitative methods are often used for exploration, rather than to test an existing assumption or hypothesis (Ritchie, Lewis, Nicholls, & Ormston, 2013), forming specific research questions prior to beginning is not as necessary as in quantitative settings. Instead, qualitative studies can be classified according to the "function" of the study, a framework for which is outlined in Table 5.1.

The second point relates to causality. Especially in the contexts of assessment and evaluation, establishing a causal relationship between a program and student outcomes might seem like the most appealing question to pursue. However, causality is a complex issue in education and across social science research. As we discuss later in this chapter in relation to methodology, addressing causal questions requires a rigorous methodological plan. Even with elaborate methods, complex analyses, and supportive results, you might not be able to make causal claims from your AER project.

Self-assessment—Choosing Your Research Questions: What questions do you want to explore in your AER project? Where do these fall in the frameworks identified in Table 5.1? Why is it that the quantitative or qualitative approach you selected is the best way of addressing these questions?

Table 5.1
TYPES OF "RESEARCH QUESTIONS" IN QUANTITATIVE AND QUALITATIVE RESEARCH DESIGNS

Increasing Complexity

Quantitative[1]	*Qualitative*[2]
Descriptive questions describe the existence or amount of a phenomenon. • E.g., "What proportion of our students demonstrate low self-efficacy in socially diverse situations?" • Serve to provide an understanding, simplification of data.	*Contextual studies* provide an overall understanding of a setting, behavior, or phenomenon. • E.g., "What are the experiences of students who visit the tutoring center? • Evidence from interviews could describe the extent to which certain attitudes exist among students.
Relational questions examine associations among variables. • E.g., "Is participation in social diversity programs related to students' self-efficacy in social situations?" • Demonstrate indications (though not conclusive evidence) of program impact or effectiveness.	*Explanatory studies* explain why certain phenomena occur. • E.g., "What factors elicit use of the tutoring center?" • Evidence from interviews could identify various social, attitudinal, or motivational factors.
Causal questions examine a direct connection between program participation and student outcomes. • E.g., "Do social diversity programs improve students' self-efficacy in social situations?" • Requires rigorous methodology that is typically infeasible in practice.	*Evaluative studies* examine the effectiveness of program, experience, or other intervention. • E.g., "What lessons from the tutoring fostered students' academic success?" • Evidence from interviews could connect students' experiences, or compare attendees to non-attendees.
	Generative studies contribute to a theory about behavior, processes, or other phenomena. • Integrates components of contextual, explanatory, and evaluative studies. • Relevant in assessment contexts by helping to build a theory of program effectiveness, possibly contributing to future improvements.

1. Trochim, Donnelly, & Arora, 2015
2. Ritchie, Lewis, Nicholls, & Ormston, 2013

Data Collection

You have decided on a quantitative or qualitative stance; you have identified the context, outcomes, goals, and research questions or problem to address. Now you can identify the research design, methodology, data sources, and analyses to be used.

If the research question is the *"what"* we want to learn, the methodology is the *"how"* we should go about learning. There are a variety of methodologies that can be employed and various ways in which those methods can be conceptualized and organized. For example, in their text on educational research, Check and Schutt (2011) identify at least six forms of methodology. Cohen, Manion, and Morrison (2013) describe eight "styles" of educational research. Rather than exhaustively explore all those approaches, our goal is to help you learn broad concepts that will guide you in identifying, comparing, and contrasting various methodologies.

Understanding Variables

Using a quantitative approach, you may elect to ask causal research questions, knowing the difficulty one can encounter when seeking to make causal claims. One of the biggest reasons for this difficulty starts with *control* of the design. Control refers to the ability to establish various desired settings of a study as well as eliminate undesired settings. The extent to which this can happen determines whether your study can be classified as a true (or "controlled") experiment, a field or quasi-experiment, or a natural experiment.

In order to describe these various settings, it is worth taking a moment to define some terminology. Factors that occur in any study are referred to as "variables," and generally speaking, there are four types of variables worth mentioning. The first two are *independent* and *dependent* variables. Independent variables are those factors or conditions that are to be compared or manipulated in a study, and these should not be influenced by other factors. Dependent variables are the outcomes of interest that we want to observe and are a result of those independent factors.

For example, if we want to study the effect of a residence life program on students' feelings of social belonging, participation in the program would be the independent variable because it is the factor that would be independent among participants. Social belonging would be the dependent variable because this is the factor we believe would change based upon students' participation in the residence life program.

The third and fourth variables (factors) are confounding and control variables. Confounding variables are factors outside of the observed independent variables that could explain changes or differences in the dependent variable. For example, if we observed that participants in the residence life program had higher feelings of social belonging than those who didn't, the results could also be explained by preexisting differences in social belonging. If students who were already very socially engaged felt more comfortable attending a residence life program, the post-program differences would be *confounded* by preprogram social belonging. Thus, including preprogram social belonging as a *control* variable, would account for any impact it might have on the dependent variable. There are several ways control variables can be addressed through both the design of a study and in the ways we analyze results. Reference to this fact are revisited throughout the remainder of the chapter. First, however, let's discuss the way that initial control determines the type of "experiment" we're trying to conduct.

Experiments: True, Quasi, and Natural

As mentioned, nearly any AER study can be classified as a true (or "controlled") experiment, a field or quasi-experiment, or a natural experiment. The key difference among these is simply the amount of control the "researcher" has over the study. The aspirational standard for most social science research is the "true" or "controlled" experiment in which researchers manipulate nearly all settings and conditions. Consider the previous residence life example. In a true experiment, a researcher would have control over the independent variable—notably, the ability to assign students to either participate in the program or not (or even to participate in another program). Ideally, this assignment would be done at random, so that any significant, confounding differences (e.g., preprogram social belonging) should theoretically be distributed equally across participants and nonparticipants. This is why *random assignment* is such an important component of any AER effort, as it has the potential to minimize the effect of confounding variables on observations made in the study.

In education, the true experiment is often unobtainable because it is practically impossible to assign a student to participate in a residence life program. It is nearly impossible to force a student who wouldn't participate to do so, and equally difficult to prevent an interested student from participating. There are also ethical limitations. If a program has promise to promote student success or learning, withholding support from students would be undesirable. As is explained below, the residence life example could end being a "field experiment" or a "natural experiment," depending on the level of control available to the researcher.

In many instances, educators work under the auspices of *quasi-experimental designs,* or *field experiments,* in which they do not have the ability to determine certain independent variables, such as assigning group membership because they are often working with intact groups. Any confounding variables are controlled for or manipulated as best as possible. In the residence life example, one might seek to measure the pre-existing social belonging of both participants and nonparticipants so that the confounding variable could be accounted for when comparing results.

In comparison to experiments that allow for control of independent variables and confounding variables, as well as and quasi-experiments in which there is a limited ability to control independent variables, natural experiments occur in settings where observation is taking place, and the researcher has essentially no ability to influence the setting, measurement, or process of the environment. Nevertheless, natural experiments still seek to compare across two groups (e.g., a "treatment" and a "control" group), but this is predetermined rather than prescribed by the researcher (e.g., comparing first-generation and continuing-generation students). This might also take place when a study is using historical data, such as the retention rates of students at an institution over the last several years.

What does all this mean for student affairs professionals? Ultimately, the goal of AER is to determine the effect of some intervention (e.g., program, activity) on a student outcome (e.g., retention, sense of belonging, engagement). If we observe a difference between those students who engage with student affairs initiatives and those who do not, we have to determine to what extent we can actually infer that such differences were because of something we (as student affairs professionals) did, or some other, confounding factor.

Naturalistic Studies

The experimental paradigm is useful when we have a reasonable understanding of students, interventions, and the ways in which they will interact to produce intended outcomes. However, there are many opportunities when developing new programs or initiatives or modifying existing programs in which it is essential to take a deeper dive into the lived experience of participants. Student affairs professionals may seek a deeper understanding of the student experience in order to establish or confirm a theory of action. In these cases, the early identification of independent, dependent, confounding, and control variables is not warranted given the approach to exploration of experiences. Qualitative research also offers specific methods of inquiry that could allow one to achieve these goals.

Naturalistic and ethnographic studies allow a researcher to understand students, their experiences, and the complex interaction with their environment—including changes in the environment because of the students' presence. According to Cohen et al. (2013), naturalistic inquiry acknowledges that the "educational world is a messy place, full of contradictions, richness, complexity, connectedness, conjunctions, and disjunctions" (p. 167). When taking this approach to assessment, evaluation, and research, clearly qualitative approaches—which allow for the consideration of rich, individualized sources of information— seem appropriate. Some common designs that are used in such studies include case studies, biographies, and ethnographies.

In a *case study* one seeks to study both what is happening and the context in which it is happening. While this can be broadly defined, examples could include the consideration of institutional context (e.g., a recent major event on campus) or current events (e.g., The Black Lives Matter Movement) while also studying the experiences of a student, the process of a program, and the interaction between the two. When such questions are of interest, but such phenomena are not readily quantifiable, naturalistic approaches are well-suited.

While case studies examine an entire process in context, *biographies* take an individualized approach. Think of two students who come to new student orientation at a large, flagship university. One student is the first in the family to go to college, while the other student had grandparents, parents, and siblings all attend the institution. In trying to understand how each student experiences orientation, it is essential to consider prior life and school experiences, personal perceptions, and social norms that influence that student's orientation experience, including what they learn and take away from the experience. Biographical approaches are designed to do just that: consider the breadth and depth of an individual's perspectives, and how that shapes individual experience and outcomes.

Finally, *ethnographies* are similar to biographies in their efforts to consider norms, values, and other background characteristics, yet different in that they consider a group of people rather than an individual. An ethnographic study of orientation might look at first-generation students as a whole, rather than a biographical approach that looks at an individual.

As you can see, case studies, biographies, and ethnographies allow for the researcher to take into consideration a wide array of factors—both intended and unconsidered—to describe a phenomenon in great depth. However, you might wonder what the results look like in both the experimental and naturalistic studies. The means by which we summarize the findings of a study—which can include numeric data, summarizing text or narratives, and other forms of results—are the focus of the next section.

Self-assessment—Choosing Your Study Design: What design do you think is most appropriate for your research question(s)? What are its strengths in answering your questions, especially in the context you've identified? What are some of the practical challenges to implementing this design (e.g., getting students to participate, resources needed)?

Sources of Data

We progress further into the development of an AER project by moving beyond the context, outcomes, goals, and methods into the data that will form our results. Note that we use the term "data" here (and throughout most of this chapter) to simply refer to information. That is, while "data" often refers to quantitative findings—that is, numbers, statistics, and so on—it can also refer to qualitative information—

text, narratives, and summaries that articulate findings in a non-numeric way. Making an informed decision about the best data is made easier by answering all of the questions we have addressed to this point. In what context is the study taking place? What are the important outcomes you want to address? How will we examine these outcomes? If these questions have been answered well, identifying the appropriate data sources should be relatively straightforward.

However, it is occasionally the case in practice that AER begins with data. You may have access to historical data, or to an assessment that is used for another purpose but is somewhat related to your study. It has been our experience that these are the cases in which debates about approaches and data sources often arise. As most measures and methods are built for a particular use, if your context, outcomes, goals, and methods align with that use, then using that data source (or sources) is often a logical choice. Misalignment between one or more of these things can threaten the ability to conduct your study or certainly to be confident in your results.

Quantitative Data

Donald Kirkpatrick (1979, 1994) presented a four-fold framework for evaluating job-training programs and which has excellent parallels for AER in student affairs. The value of this approach is the ability to identify, compare, and contrast various data sources commonly encountered in student affairs contexts. These four levels of data are reactions, learning, behavior, and results.

Reactions. "Reactions," or students' self-reported evaluations of the program, are usually the first and most common way we can examine a program's impact. Following a program, we might survey students as to whether they learned something or if they found the program to be effective. While students' perceptions of their experience are a valuable part of understanding program impact, they are simply one perspective, and one impacted by many factors other than the quality, effectiveness, or impact of the program (for a brief review of some of the challenges with self-report, see Paulhus and Vazire, 2007). Moreover, as you look to address larger and broader audiences, additional data—beyond just reports of effectiveness—may be required.

Learning. The second level of data is learning, or the acquisition of the knowledge, skill, or disposition that is the target of the program.

When a program is conducted in the cocurricular context, we often ask students the extent to which the program was effective in developing an outcome without actually administering a more direct measure of development. For example, consider a new student orientation program intended to foster students' help-seeking attitudes and skills. At the conclusion of orientation, we may ask students, "To what extent did your orientation help you understand the resources that are available on campus?" This would be classified as reactions-level data, as students are self-reporting the effectiveness of the program. Or, we could provide a knowledge-based test, asking students to identify which resources are appropriate for certain circumstances (e.g., where to go when in need of tutoring). This would be considered learning-level data, as we are focusing on more direct indications of the learning outcomes of the program.

Behavior. Kirkpatrick's third level of data deals with how students behave after leaving the program, and whether the knowledge, skills, attitudes, and behaviors are applied. Consider a program that works with students who have had alcohol violations during college, and seeks to foster healthy social behaviors and decision making in the presence of alcohol. Students are taught to make a plan for getting home, to count the number of drinks, and to avoid drinks from an untrusted source. For reactions-level data, we might ask students if they thought the program was helpful or effective (reactions). We could then test if students can identify the appropriate strategy for a given social situation (learning). After students complete the program—perhaps two to three months later—we could ask them the extent to which they'd used the strategies learned in the program while at various social events. This use of this information would then serve as behavior-level data.

Results. Results-level data address questions related to the ultimate goals or desired impact of a program. Results can often be identified by answers to questions such as, "Why do you want students to learn these skills?" or, "If students used what they learned in your program, what would the impact be?" In academic settings, results-level data are also some of the more common metrics used across our institutions, such as retention or graduation rates, or grade-point averages, though other factors could be considered outside of the institution or even after students graduate. For example, one result of an internship program could be student job placement rates.

Kirkpatrick's framework provides a logical sequence of data to support a demonstration of program effectiveness. With a thorough array of data, student affairs professionals can confidently examine program impact by showing student perceptions of effectiveness (reactions), evidence of student learning (learning), changes in student behavior (behavior), and, accordingly, an impact on other metrics of value to multiple stakeholders, such as retention rates (results).

Qualitative Data Sources

As shown, quantitative data sources provide numeric summaries of student behavior, attitudes, skills, and other factors; qualitative data sources, however, must provide the opportunity to capture a variety of individual, situational, and contextual factors. These sources typically involve somewhat open-ended artifacts that can be flexible enough to describe an array of phenomena. In student affairs settings, some of the more common sources of qualitative data are observations, interviews, essays, and other constructed pieces of student work (e.g., a portfolio).

Just as in quantitative settings, the integration of multiple qualitative sources can also be beneficial. As Mason (2002) points out, several pieces of evidence can help to provide multiple perspectives on various characteristics. For example, observing a student's interactions with peers could provide different information about their social integration than an interview with that same student. Moreover, multiple data sources can support a more conclusive statement about results, especially when independent sources agree on findings. Finally, multiple data sources might be necessary to capture different AER components or to answer multiple research questions. While interviews, for example, could capture the student experience, they might not capture the program setting or context sought in a case study.

Self-assessment—Identifying Data Sources: Given all the context and design choices you've made thus far, what data sources do you think best address your research question? At what level (i.e., reactions, learning, behavior, or results) do these data exist? How might you incorporate data from multiple levels (ideally all of them) to address your research question?

Data Analyses

Given the wide array of data sources described previously, it might seem like the number of possible methods for analyzing those sources would be immense. Indeed, there are many ways quantitative and qualitative data can be examined, summarized, and reported. We present some of the major themes and approaches in both areas, but the underlying lesson for student affairs professionals is that decisions about data analyses should be aligned with previous components of the study's context, outcome, and goals. These will guide decisions about data analysis, and contribute to the overall success of the effort by addressing the goals of importance (and avoiding efforts to address goals that aren't important).

Quantitative Data Analyses

Your data sources could include any combination of students' demonstrations of knowledge, behaviors, and/or reactions that occur as a result of your program. Yet determining the appropriate analyses will ultimately depend on whether you are interested in answering questions about the description of these sources, the relationships among variables, or the causal nature of observations.

Descriptive statistics. Returning to our previous discussion, descriptive questions will lead to the use of descriptive statistics, which provide simple summaries about the participants and the measures included in your study. They also form the basis for many other quantitative analyses (as you will soon see). There are generally three types of descriptive statistics: distributions, central tendency, and dispersion.

Distribution statistics show how many units fall at each category or level of a variable. Listing the number of students who received an A, B, C, and so on, in a student success course, for example, would display the distribution of course grades.

Measures of central tendency are intended to provide a representation of a variable across a group of students. For example, providing the average high school GPA of students enrolling in new student orientation can use a single statistic to better represent the larger group. However, "average" can be statistically described in several ways, most commonly mean (the numeric average), median (the middle score in a distribution of ordered, numeric values), or mode (the most commonly occurring value in a set).

Measures of central tendency summarize multiple data points into one value; in contrast, measures of dispersion show how representative that score might be. In other words, how widely spread are values about that measure of central tendency? The two most common measures of dispersion are the range and standard deviation of scores. Range simply shows the distance between the highest and lowest values (e.g., "scores ranged from 24 to 78"). Standard deviation is a statistic that represents how much scores, on average, differ from the mean.

To exhaustively discuss the methods, computations, and potential presentation of descriptive statistics is beyond our scope, yet there are two important points to make about them. First, descriptive statistics help in reporting AER results by summarizing and representing the data. Rather than listing the high school GPA of every student in orientation, we can present the mean and standard deviation, which demonstrate the central tendency and distribution of scores in a far more efficient way.

One of the other advantages of descriptive statistics is that they give the researcher a better understanding of the data. For example, if you were to calculate the mean high school GPA of orientation registrants to be 3.90 (on a traditional 4-point scale), you would quickly know that the group was, on average, rather academically prepared. Or, if you were to find an average score of 3.0, but a range of 1.0-4.0, you could then understand that the group of orientation students varied widely in their level of academic preparation. Creating graphical displays of raw data (e.g., histograms, scatter plots) can allow you to better understand larger groups of data before progressing to inferential methods.

Inferential statistics. As questions become more complex—moving from descriptive inquiries to relational inquiries—so do analytic methods. Relational questions are associated with the use of *inferential statistics,* which move beyond simply describing and summarizing data to making inferences or claims about the students you observe. The two most common inferences sought in AER deal with relation and comparison. When relating variables, we want to know if a change in one (usually our independent variable) coincides with change in another (usually our dependent variable). Is engagement in cocurricular programs and services related to students' sense of belonging? Does the number of visits to the tutoring center relate to students' grades in class?

In these cases, the goal of *inferring* a relationship between two variables is to support or explore an *inference* that aligns with the AER study. In order to calculate this relationship, the most basic metric is the correlation, though much more complex methods, often based on correlational analyses, are often used. Correlations measure the extent to which change in one variable relates to change in another variable. Correlations range from −1 to 1, with positive values indicating that, as one variable increases or decreases, so does the other. A negative correlation indicates an inverse relationship; as one variable increases, the other decreases. The higher the magnitude of the correlation, the stronger the relationship between the variables. That is, a correlation of −1 means that, in every case, as one variable decreases, the other increases. (Note that in more complex studies, correlations may also be included as part of descriptive statistics when they convey underlying characteristics of the data.)

There are two important, practical notes to be made about correlations. First, correlations rarely approach values of 1 or -1. As an example, in a large-scale study of first-year retention and grade point averages, Robbins et al. (2004) found several significant predictors of student outcomes, but rarely did any predictor exceed .4 in value. Additionally, it is important to note that correlation is not a direct indicator of a causal relationship between two variables. Correlations can occur for several noncausal reasons, but perhaps the most notable example is a "spurious" correlation, whereby two variables are related as a result of a third, unobserved, explanatory variable (for some interesting examples, see Duncan, 2015).

A second common inference refers to differences among groups. For example, we might compare the sense of belonging among participants and nonparticipants in a peer-mentoring program. We could also compare the class grades of students who attended tutoring to those who didn't.

Simply calculating the correlation or the mean difference is not an inferential process. Comparing the mean GPA of students who went to the tutoring center (e.g., 3.2) to those who didn't (e.g., 2.9) doesn't make a claim about that difference—it is simply descriptive: The difference is 0.3 grade points. What is required to make an *inference* about that finding is to determine whether that difference is meaningful, or as is commonly used in social science settings: "statistically significant." It is only in determining this difference as statistically significant or not that we can make an inference about our finding.

One method for determining significance is through statistical significance testing. Statistical significance is designed to determine whether a result occurs due to fluctuations in observations based on the sample(s) we've observed, or represents a true difference. Let's say we wanted to compare the average height of people in North Dakota and South Dakota. Since it would be logistically infeasible to measure everyone in those states, we decide to find 100 people in each state and measure their height. If we found that our North Dakotan sample had an average height of 5'7" and our South Dakotan sample had an average height of 5'8", could we reasonably *infer* that South Dakotans are taller? One of the challenges to this inference is the sample we took. If we took a different sample of 100 people from each state, it is quite reasonable to assume that we might find something different—perhaps even the opposite finding.

Significance testing is used to compare the finding (in this case, the mean difference between our samples) to the expected distribution of means to determine how that difference compares to random fluctuation between samples. The user then calculates a likelihood, the p value, that indicates the probability of finding a result when those differences do not actually exist between the two populations. Generally, researchers set a standard of 5% for this error, though that level can be changed at the discretion of the researcher. Thus, the common practice is labeling a finding of "$p < .05$" as "statistically significant."

In addition to significance testing, which tells us how comparing an observed finding to the likelihood of finding nothing at all, we calculate effect sizes that tell us the magnitude of an observation. Effect sizes quantify the magnitude of a relationship or score difference. In correlational studies, we can often look at the size of the correlation value. (This is reasonable because correlations, regardless of how a variable is measured, are always on the scale of −1 to 1.) When examining mean differences, Cohen's (1992) d is a commonly used metric that compares the size of the effect to the standard deviation (again providing differences on a common scale). The use of effect sizes allows researchers to compare findings across similar studies.

In this section, we've covered many concepts that are rather complex. Our goal is to simply provide an overview of key issues to consider and questions to address when designing and conducting AER studies. When doing so, consulting appropriate research, statistics, or data analysis texts (e.g., Cohen, Manion, & Morrison, 2013; Trochim, Donnelly, & Arora, 2015) will be necessary. Perhaps more importantly, consulting and collaborating with colleagues (e.g., assessment and institutional research staff) with expertise in these areas will likely increase the receptivity of your work to various audiences. Ultimately, as a student affairs professional, you might not be required to be an expert in data analysis or statistics, but identifying the key components of an effective analytic method could be incredibly helpful in conducting assessment, evaluation, and research of student affairs programs.

A Note about Causality. While we have addressed descriptive and relational questions, we have yet to address analyses that can help support causal research questions. In the case where causal claims are sought, it is not the analysis that will need to change. Rather, and as we've addressed before, only the set-up and control of the study can support such an inference.

Qualitative Data Analysis

Quantitative analyses involve summarizing and interpreting numbers; qualitative data analyses involve additional steps to organize, break down, and infer meaning from the data source. There is an extensive body of work on the philosophy, research, and science supporting practices to summarize and make meaning from qualitative sources. For a more thorough examination of key processes, we recommend LeCompte and Preissle (1993), who provide a thorough, seven-step process for qualitative data analysis. Here, we provide some general guidelines—based on that work—to help outline some broad, necessary steps.

The first step is to break down, identify, and group the elements within your data source. For example, consider a study of students' sense of belonging using interviews conducted after new student orientation. As you examine the interview transcripts, there could be a large amount of text. In order to simplify the text, you could identify all the words related to students' sense of belonging (e.g., "welcomed," "isolated," "family"). Or, you could use statements as the "unit of analysis." You would then want to group those statements according to commonalities (e.g., "attitudes toward other students," "attitudes toward faculty," "feelings of alienation").

Once you have created a set of data elements, you can begin to identify relationships among them. For example, you may observe that students who identified with other students were also more likely to express feelings of belonging. You would also want to hypothesize why you think these relationships occur, based on the evidence at hand. For example—based on your observations, or other research you've considered—you might hypothesize that connections with peers might drive or at least be a key part of a student's more general sense of belonging.

Because qualitative study is based largely in the perspectives of the researcher, it is important to be considerate of and transparent about counter cases. Thus, it is good practice to identify and explore cases in which your hypothesis does not hold. In this example, are there students with strong connections who do not also demonstrate a sense of belonging? If so, what evidence can you observe to explain these cases?

The final step is to summarize your findings by generating a model, or theory, explaining your observations. Especially in a student affairs context, in which qualitative approaches can be used to develop an understanding of how a program influences change in students, this stage is critical for contributing to future planning, development, or additional AER. What insights have your observations provided? What future questions would you like to explore? What does this mean for your context (e.g., program, institution, student population)?

Validity, Reliability, and Fairness

Once you have determined the type(s) of data to be used, it is important to examine the quality of the evidence gathered. In quantitative studies, this is typically framed through the foundational concepts of validity, reliability, and fairness. Similarly, qualitative studies may discuss these concepts through related terms such as transferability or trustworthiness. These concepts, whether framed through a quantitative or qualitative perspective, are especially important when measuring student learning and development in a way that makes an inference about unobserved constructs (e.g., self-efficacy, sense of belonging, motivation).

Quantitative Settings

Validity, reliability, and fairness, which are concepts most often applied to quantitative data, are thoroughly addressed through both current standards in educational and psychological fields (American Educational Research Association [AERA], American Psychological Association [APA], & National Council on Measurement in Education [NCME], 2014) and theoretical foundations (Kane, 2001, 2013; Messick, 1989). Perhaps the most important statement to be made about reliability, validity, and fairness is that they are not inherent characteristics of any measure. Professionals will occasionally refer to a test or instrument as being "validated," as if to suggest that a study or body of research can cement the quality of a measure in perpetuity. An important insight to be taken from this is that your practical use of these assessments offers opportunities to add to a larger body of research, meanwhile strengthening the evidence for the claims you make regarding the outcomes of your program.

Validity generally refers to the extent that evidence has been provided to support the use of a measure for that purpose (AERA, APA, & NCME, 2014). As Benson (1996) demonstrates (again, based on previous theoretical work by Messick, 1989, and Kane, 2001, 2013), there are three common forms of validity evidence.

1. **Content validity** evidence demonstrates alignment between assessment items or tasks and established models of the theory or domain that the measure is intended to address. This could be gathered by having subject matter experts' rate or articulate item-theory alignment. It is important to ensure that an appropriate amount of relevant content exists within your assessment. Using the example of a study habits questionnaire, you may question the content validity if there were no task, questions, or items within the assessment that address the amount of time spent studying.

2. **Structural validity** evidence is demonstrated when the constructs assessed relate to one another as expected. For example, relationships among items designed to measure the same construct, as well as lack of relation among items intended to measure distinct constructs, would represent structural validity evidence. Consider the development of a measure of study habits for a tutoring program. High overall scores on this assessment would indicate better study habits, and lower overall scores would indicate worse study habits. In this assessment you could imagine developing survey items addressing the amount of time spent studying, strategies used to study, and so on—such that

responses are positively related to the overall score. The more time spent studying, the more likely your score would reflect better study habits. On the other hand, you could also include items measuring procrastination behaviors. Responses indicating more procrastination behaviors would be negatively related to better study skills. These relationships could be predicted by theory or by practical understanding of study habits. However, if items do not relate to one another and to the total score in predicted ways (e.g., more time spent studying was more closely related to poor study habits) then there may be reason to question the structural validity of the assessment.

3. **Criterion-related or external validity** evidence is demonstrated when the construct measured relates to external variables in expected ways. For example, an assessment designed to measure study skills should have stronger correlations with similar measures, such as measures of organization, and weaker relationships with unrelated measures, such as those of self-efficacy. Predictive relationships with relevant results-level variables, such as retention rates or GPA, could also be considered criterion-related validity evidence.

Reliability generally refers to the replicability or consistency of scores. When measuring a student on a given skill or behavior, such as test anxiety, a desirable characteristic of that measure would be that it produces consistent results. Hypothetically speaking, imagine that we could ask a student to complete the text anxiety measure, then give that same student the same assessment again (without effects of fatigue, practice, etc.). The extent to which the scores on the two testing situations agree is an indication of score reliability.

Reliability can be estimated in a variety of ways, though two popular methods include test-retest reliability, whereby a measure is administered multiple times to determine if scores are consistent, and internal consistency reliability, whereby individual item responses are compared to determine if scores are consistent within a measure. From the perspective of a student affairs professional, understanding the underlying concepts and key distinctions of various reliability estimates is less crucial than understanding the importance of reliability and ensuring that any instrument used in an assessment process has sufficient reliability evidence (e.g., consult a practical reference such as Cicchetti, 1994).

If validity refers to evidence of a measure, score, or data source to support a claim or argument, then fairness is evidenced by data showing that such claims are equally representative across key groups of students, particularly traditionally underserved or underrepresented groups. For example, if two groups of students are truly equal in self-efficacy, but a measure consistently shows that one group is lower than another, that measure would be considered bias, because it has misrepresented one group. In other words, differences in test scores according to group membership (e.g., by gender or race/ethnicity) are not an immediate sign of bias, as they might suggest actual differences in a construct. Certainly, fairness is a key issue in assessment and testing, and more thorough discussions of fairness in a wide array of contexts are available (e.g., Kane, 2010; Reynolds & Ramsay, 2003).

Qualitative Settings

Several authors have considered how the concepts of validity, reliability, and fairness might apply—or fail to apply—in qualitative settings (e.g., Creswell & Miller, 2000; Golafshani, 2003; Hammersly, 1992). One important example is the use of inter-rater reliability to ensure that qualitative data are coded and organized consistently (Armstrong, Gosling, Weinman, & Marteau, 1997). Generally, there is agreement that some tenets of validity, reliability, and fairness can positively impact qualitative research, though in some cases those concepts are applied differently.

For example, rather than thinking about reliability as replicability, it could be considered as an issue of data quality, or "trustworthiness" (Golafshani, 2003). This leads directly to similar concepts of validity—ensuring that qualitative data support the conclusions we hope to make. Hammersly (1992) notes that several tactics can ensure this, including that the sample is representative of the students to which we hope to speak, that the setting of the study allows for sufficient observation of the relevant factors, and that our results accurately summarize the data in its entirety.

Regardless of terminology and theoretical stances, what is key to remember in any educational research, assessment, and evaluation context is that we should be seeking to ensure the integrity of our AER project at each stage of the process. Have we worked to ensure that our data—quantitative or qualitative—are free of errors and represent what they should? Have we worked to consider different perspectives or explanations for the phenomena we observe? Lastly, have we made sure that the evidence we have provided reasonably supports the claims we made? These are the central questions that ensure reliability and validity, regardless of context or approach.

How to Apply This Competency

Throughout this chapter, we have attempted to take some rather complex concepts and boil them down to the key practical lessons for student affairs practitioners. As you apply these competencies, however, we would encourage you to keep three key principles in mind.

First, we have attempted to emphasize the importance of planning. You will likely encounter situations where a great deal of planning is not possible. You may have to employ existing data sources that don't align with your ideal methods or design. The only student samples available might not fully support the comparisons you'd like to make. You might not be able to observe certain variables that are key to understanding students' experiences. However, if you strive to begin with the context, goals, and research questions of your AER effort, and align the methodology and data collection that best meets those demands, your effort will be more effective.

The second principle is to use whatever resources you have available. We have cited other resources throughout this chapter that could augment and elaborate on the information we have provided (e.g., Cohen et al., 2013; Check & Schutt, 2011; Creswell, 2014; Ritchie, Lewis, Nicholls, & Ormston, 2013; Trochim et al., 2015). These can be valuable guides to expand your own understanding and skills in the areas of qualitative, quantitative, and mixed methods approaches (i.e., those that employ both qualitative and quantitative tactics).

Few student affairs professionals are experts in methodology, data analysis, or validity theory. While this chapter and other resources can expand your understanding, collaborating with others can contribute significantly to the effectiveness of your AER effort. Institutional researchers, social science faculty, and other student affairs practitioners can help to augment your strengths in these studies.

Lastly, we would encourage you to constantly learn, iterate, and improve your AER practice. Even with excellent planning, problems in collection and analysis of data can always arise. Or, an established plan may not provide sufficient evidence to address a research question. Perhaps most positively, one study might only raise additional questions to be answered in future endeavors. While assessment and evaluation are often placed on a cycle within colleges and universities, these efforts are rarely repetitive in practice.

Case Study from Student Affairs

While this chapter contains several examples that are designed to provide a practical context for theoretical context, it can also be help-ful to apply the strategies and their possible outcomes in a novel set-ting. Table 5.2 highlights and outlines some of the key decision points.

Table 5.2
DATA COLLECTION, METHODOLOGY, AND ANALYSIS DECISION TREE

Question	*Factors to Consider*	*Possible Outcomes*	
What is the context?	- Stakes - Scope - Audience	- Assessment - Evaluation - Research	
What is the research approach?	- Theoretical stance - Data sources available (numeric data vs. open-ended) - Nature of study (exploratory vs. confirmatory)	- Quantitative - Qualitative	
What are your research questions/goals?	- Familiarity with the setting, data - Goals of the study - Level of control over study variable	*Quantitative* - Descriptive - Relational - Causal	*Qualitative* - *Contextual* - *Explanatory* - *Evaluative* - *Generative*
What methodology will you employ?	- Level of control - Groups being observed - Level of phenomena (individual vs. group)	*Quantitative* - Natural experiment - Field experiment - True experiment	*Qualitative* - Case study - Biography - Ethnography
What type(s) of data will be used?	- Stakes, scope, audience - Context - Access to students	*Quantitative* - Reactions - Learning - Behavior - Results	*Qualitative* - Interviews - Essays - Student work

Using the concepts and tools discussed in this chapter regarding methodology, data collection, and data analysis, we have laid the foundation for Chapter 6, which will focus on interpreting, reporting, and using results. That chapter explores how to leverage the results of your findings to better support your desired outcomes.

Chapter 6

INTERPRETING, REPORTING, AND USING RESULTS

R. LORRAINE BERNOTSKY

This chapter will focus on interpreting data, reporting findings, and utilizing results in ways that support learning in the cocurricular. Knowing how to interpret and present data in ways that communicate a story is critical to the work of student affairs professionals. Data can be intimidating in raw form, but for most people, data make a compelling case when woven together in a seamless way that is accessible and easy to comprehend. While qualitative data tends to be easier for people to comprehend at face value, using numbers to tell a story can provide a context for the initiatives or goals you want to achieve. Numbers can also strengthen one's ability to advocate for additional dollars to support programming even in the face of competing demands for resources that are common to all institutional settings. In order to be successful, student affairs professionals need to develop several key skills and competencies. According to the *ACPA/NASPA Professional Competencies Rubrics* (2016, p. 16), professionals should:

- Know how to interpret data in practical terms that are relevant to the institutional context.
- Demonstrate an ability to present results concisely in reports that are useful to a variety of audiences.
- Be able to use findings to make informed decisions and to align resources.

- Demonstrate a disposition to collaborate, which includes representing findings accurately and fairly and sharing interpretations with stakeholders, including students.

Interpretation: Context and Key Considerations

While the phrase did not originate with him, Mark Twain is generally credited with popularizing the statement that there are three kinds of lies: lies, damned lies, and statistics (Twain, 1906, p. 512). In its popular usage today, the implication is that the analysis and interpretation of data that is at the heart of statistics is at best more art than science and at worst, nothing more than a magic trick, intended to mislead and confuse an audience through numerical manipulation rather than sleight of hand. Of course, there is an alternative view, one that recognizes the power of a narrative that we can build with the well-reasoned use of data, providing the framework for a transparent exploration of factors related to student learning and success. Improving the success of our students by understanding and being able to explain to others the variables and interventions that affect that success is critical to the work of student affairs professionals.

Context

Promoting student success is central to all universities. Student learning outcomes and student success goals are part of the day-to-day vocabulary of institutions, yet the lenses through which student success is viewed has an impact on the way various constituencies define student success. As Rhine, Martinez-Saenz, and Davenport (2012) note, legislatures tend to define student success in terms of retention and graduation rates, while universities tend to define success as academic achievement, involvement in cocurricular and social life, as well as metrics that are congruent with legislative definitions. Faculty and staff tend to define student success in terms of learning, growth, and development, while students themselves tend to define success as achieving their goals as they have defined them. In this context, there is a dizzying array of elements related to student success and student learning. The challenge for the student affairs professional is to understand not only this broad context of definitions, but also the elements related to definitions of student success and learning that are part of your local institutional culture.

The level of support, interest, or skepticism you may find at your institution for the work of student affairs professionals in assessing and evaluating student learning outcomes and student success is often related to the type of institution itself. Research-intensive institutions with medical schools, law schools, or other heavily graduate professional or research-focused faculty are often places where the assessment and evaluation work of student affairs professionals can flourish in relatively unbounded ways. This is because the focus of the academic affairs units is not as centered on the core elements of undergraduate student learning outcomes that are shared with general education (i.e., the AAC&U VALUE rubrics), as noted by Finney and Horst in Chapter 1.

On the other hand, at a regional comprehensive or small private institution where undergraduate students represent the overwhelming majority of enrollment, the academic affairs units are more likely to be heavily invested in the assessment and evaluation of student learning outcomes that are central to the work of both student affairs and academic affairs. While the lenses with which these divisions view student success may be different (curricular or cocurricular), the student learning outcome goals tend to overlap. In these places, it is critically important for student affairs professionals to understand the importance of collaboration and the political context of results, which will be discussed later in this chapter. In any case, connecting learning in the cocurricular to institutionally accepted learning outcomes is a useful strategy.

Another key element of context for the interpretation and presentation of findings is related to an institution's progress towards a culture of assessment (recall the discussion in Chapter 3). During the early stages of developing a culture of assessment, it is important to understand as much about what is not in the data you are analyzing as what is actually being presented. An example of this is the rationale for the criteria for a measure of success. In the early stages of developing a culture of assessment, it is common to see benchmarks or milestones noted without a rationale for why that particular benchmark has been chosen, e.g., 80% of students will report satisfaction with the quality of the advising they receive. Why is 80% the "right" benchmark? Unless the measure chosen is linked to a rationale, it is unclear why that particular level of performance is acceptable as an institutional goal. As an institution moves further along the spectrum of developing a culture of assessment, people's expertise in gathering and reporting data increases because their ability to ask the right questions and frame robust research designs increases also.

Key Considerations

There are several key elements that should be considered when engaging in the interpretation of data, including: developing data definitions, understanding nonfindings, understanding the relationship between causality and correlation, and avoiding bias in the interpretation of results.

First is the importance of data definitions. The concept of data definitions does not refer to terminology related to data analysis, such as kurtosis or homoscedasticity. Rather, the concept refers to the definitions of the variables themselves, such as student success or student engagement.

One of the most common areas of misinterpretation of findings occurs when readers assume a definition of a variable that is different from what the variable is actually measuring. This is often related to the use of multidimensional language versus unidimensional language in measurement. A multidimensional term is one where the meaning can differ from person to person. Unidimensional language, on the other hand, has one meaning. Think about the difference between saying a student has "good grades" versus saying a student has a GPA of 3.8. "Good grades" is an example of multidimensional language; the meaning varies depending on a person's perspective about what constitutes good academic performance. GPA, on the other hand, is understood to be a precise point on what is usually a four-point scale.

In the ideal world, questions about data definitions would take place as part of research design, before data are collected and analysis is completed. However, we often find ourselves needing to use data collected for the routine reporting work of a university; in those cases, a discussion about definitions is critically important to the interpretation of findings. For example, if you are doing year-to-year comparisons of student data and you are considering data related to students by race and ethnicity, it is critical to know how your institution defines URM (underrepresented minority) students and if that definition has changed over time.

A second critical element of data interpretation is understanding the importance of nonfindings. As noted by Markle and Russell in Chapter 5, a quality research design includes well-developed questions and appropriate tools for analysis. Often this process leads to findings that help us refine our practices and initiatives and/or develop better student learning goals. But what happens when the analyses we conduct result in findings that have no statistical significance? A common mistake, especially for the less-experienced professional, is to try doggedly to find some statistical test that will yield a result that is significant in order to support the hypothesis that was at the heart of the analysis in the first place.

While it is always a good idea to explore different tools for analysis if you are uncertain of what the most appropriate tools are, if you are confident in your research design and the quality of your data and your analyses are not yielding statistically significant results, it is time to think about the importance of reporting nonfindings. The temptation is to set this work aside and "start over" in the hopes of finding something important to share, but there is a loss to our collective understanding of an issue if we aren't willing to share these research "failures." As science philosopher Karl Popper famously wrote in *Conjectures and Refutations: The Growth of Scientific Knowledge,* "Refutations have often been regarded as establishing the failure of a scientist, or at least of his theory. It should be stressed that this is an inductivist error. Every refutation should be regarded as a great success. . . . Even if a new theory . . . should meet an early death, it should not be forgotten; rather its beauty should be remembered, and history should record our gratitude to it—for bequeathing to us new and perhaps still unexplained experimental facts and, with them, new problems . . ." (Popper, 1963, p. 329).

What is complicated about reporting nonfindings in the context of a university setting is that findings are often tied to funding and institutional support (or the lack thereof) related to initiatives to improving student outcomes. While the political context will be addressed later in this chapter, it is nonetheless important to report nonfindings that are related to key elements of your hypothesis. It is even more important to explore and understand why your hypothesis was not supported by the findings, because this may lead to important discoveries you had not considered.

Consider the following real-life example. A course-based learning communities pilot was launched at an institution using the hypothesis that first-year students who took two or more courses in cohorts (the course-based "learning community") would perform better academically (measured by GPA) than students who were not part of cohorts across common first-year courses. Students were randomly assigned to the pilot and in this sense the student profiles were similar across pilot and nonpilot courses. After two years of data collection, the analysis revealed that the GPAs were almost identical across the pilot and non-pilot groups. The faculty team responsible for the pilot was frustrated and abandoned the pilot, unwilling to report the findings of this apparent failure. In conversations with other colleagues much later, however, when they were willing to talk about their nonfindings, someone suggested that GPA may not be the appropriate measure to use to judge "success" as evidenced by what remained a relatively normal distribution of GPA data despite an intervention. A colleague suggested looking at retention instead as a marker of first-year student success; when they did so, the faculty team found that retention was significantly higher for the cohorts that were in the pilot than for the other students. For student affairs professionals, this will likely come as no surprise. But what the faculty team began to understand was the importance of cognitive nonacademic factors (such as feeling part of a community or a sense of belonging) on student success. Willingness to share a "failure" can often provide keen insights into what is missing from our hypotheses and can provide invaluable new knowledge to our work around student success.

There are, of course, other reasons nonfindings that may not yield key new insights should still be discussed in your report. A program may not have been designed and implemented appropriately to make an impact; the measurement tool may not have been sensitive enough to detect subtle changes; or the sample size may have been too small to demonstrate statistically significant results. In each of these cases, a discussion of the reason(s) for the nonfindings is useful, as is a discussion of other meaningful results that may not be statistically significant.

A further consideration for interpreting data is understanding the relationship between causality and correlation. In order to establish causality between two variables, three conditions at a minimum must be met: the cause must precede the effect in time, the variables must be empirically correlated (as one changes, so does the other), and the relationship cannot be explained by the introduction of a third variable (Lazarsfeld, 1959). Consider the example of shoe size and reading performance for elementary school children. We can demonstrate statistically that these two variables are empirically positively related (as one increases, so does the other). However, better reading perfor-mance is not *caused* by shoe size. Rather, a third intervening variable explains both of these increases: age. As children get older their feet get larger and their reading performance increases as they advance through elementary school. Similarly, we can demonstrate the classic example that as ice cream sales increase so does the violent crime rate. Does that mean that ice cream sales are somehow increasing violent crime rates? No, rather this correlation is spurious (washed away by a third variable) because the correlation can be explained by a third variable: warmer weather. Ice cream sales rise during the warmer times of the year, and hot weather is one of several factors that can lead to a greater incidence of crime in the summer.

Given the interconnectedness of variables related to our work around student success, it is important to recognize that there are often multiple contributing variables leading to some observed effect. In this sense, a correlation between two variables that is not spurious still does not necessarily mean that one causes the other. Demon-strating that two variables tend to occur together is a necessary but not sufficient condition for causality. Consider the example of student engagement. If we did a survey of students around their level of en-gagement in cocurricular experiences and mapped those outcomes against their GPA or retention, it would probably not surprise you to find that students who are engaged in cocurricular activities also do better on metrics related to academic success. Does this mean that en-gagement "causes" academic success? We could certainly demonstrate a positive correlation with statistical significance using data from any number of universities. But it is important to think about what other variables might also need to be considered before drawing the con-clusion that engagement in and of itself causes academic success. What if the students who tend to get involved in cocurricular experi-ences are also those who had a stronger academic profile (measured for instance by class rank or high school GPA) upon entering the uni-versity? If this were the case, it would be important to include that analysis as part of the discussion of findings from the survey in order to take into account related variables (high school class rank and GPA) that tend to be correlated with academic success.

Related to the practice of considering multiple contributing factors when presenting findings is also the commitment to avoiding bias in the interpretation of results.

While Chapter 5 provided strategies related to avoiding bias in research design, it is important to be vigilant about bias in the reporting of results as well. There is a distinction here between intentional bias and unintentional bias. The quote at the beginning of this chapter about lies, damned lies, and statistics refers to the unfortunate fact that sometimes people choose to selectively report findings in ways that support their own agendas (intentional bias). There is a clear ethical commitment expected of student affairs professionals (and all researchers) in the analysis and reporting of findings that is consistent with ACPA/NASPA professional competencies as noted in Chapter 1. But it is often the case that bias in the interpretation of findings is subtler than an obvious intent to misinform. In the context of scarce resources and advocacy, it can be tempting to select only results that show a program or initiative in the best light, rather than share results that describe the findings more representatively.

Let us say, for example, that you are in charge of an initiative meant to provide after-hours programming once a week for a semester to first-year residential students based on the hypothesis that this will increase their feelings of belonging. In order to track the frequency of engagement, you have students sign in on an iPad at the beginning of each evening and you ask a few related questions about their feelings around belonging. At the end of the semester, you analyze your results and you are pleased to find that the mean (average) number of evenings attended was 8.01 (or 53%) out of a possible 14 nights for your group of 100 students. You note that the mode (the number occurring most often), however, is one. A frequency table reveals that 40% of the students attended only once, but the remaining 60 attended a range of 12 to 14 times. Reporting a mean of 8.01 would not be inaccurate, but it would be misleading, and there is a bigger story to tell. It is not actually the case that students attended 53% of sessions. Rather, for the 60% of students who attended more than once, attendance ranged from 86% to 100%. This level of retention is a very compelling statement about the engagement of students who attended more than one session as well as the importance of engaging students beyond the first session. In addition, you would want to ensure that your analysis of survey responses around feelings of belonging distinguishes between these two groups since your hypothesis around this intervention was that engaging in after-hours activities would increase feelings of belonging.

Disclosure of key information related to your data is critical to avoiding unintentional bias. Some additional common examples of bias in the interpretation of findings include overgeneralizing findings beyond the group upon which the analysis was based and drawing conclusions that go beyond the variables that were considered in the analysis. In our example above, this could mean assuming your findings about a group of first-year students could be applied generally to all students (overgeneralizing) or using your findings to draw conclusions about elements other than feelings of belonging.

Finally, when considering the interpretation and presentation of findings, it is important to understand an institution's culture around data-informed versus data-driven decision making. As Kennedy-Phillips and Ross note in Chapter 3, a telling characteristic of a data-informed institutional culture is a commitment to data literacy at all levels. If your institution does not exhibit this characteristic, it is important to determine if the culture is more data-driven than data-informed. Many institutions start out on the path towards a culture of assessment as data-driven, interpreting results rigidly and leaving little room for nuance or the exploration of alternate hypotheses and having made little progress on institution-wide data literacy.

For institutions at this stage, it is incumbent on the student affairs professional to engage in education around data-informed decision making as part of the process of interpreting and reporting findings. What would this look like at an institution that has not fully evolved into a data-informed rather than a data-driven culture? It may be the case that emphasizing the interconnectedness of findings (multiple variables contributing to academic success, for example) provides an opportunity to educate colleagues about correlation and causality that would not necessarily be needed at an institution that has evolved more fully into a data-informed culture. In this way, taking institutional context into account has an impact on the way in which findings should be presented.

Presentation of Results: Methodological Considerations and Reporting Style

While the preceding section focused on institutional context, it is equally important to understand both the purpose of your report and the audience(s) you are addressing when presenting results. There are multiple factors to consider when deciding how best to prepare and present your results; above all, you must be committed to representing findings accurately. Transparency around this principle is critical and the traditional comprehensive report is a useful model to illustrate this commitment. The common elements of a comprehensive report include:

- Discussion of the context for the study or the analysis, including the purpose, hypotheses, or questions that are explored.
- Method(s) of data gathering (e.g., survey data, institutional research data, focus group data, Integrated Postsecondary Education Data System [IPEDS] data) as well as the methodological approach (qualitative, quantitative, or mixed methods).
- Discussion of the strengths and limitations of both the data and methodology employed, including a discussion of missing data if appropriate (see below).
- Presentation of the findings (as well as nonfindings where applicable), including highlights and lessons learned.
- Recommendations for follow-up action or further exploration, including a brief justification for each.

The section that follows focuses first on the content of the traditional comprehensive report and then on considerations of style as well as other types of brief reports.

Methodological Considerations

Bearing in mind the differences between assessment, program review, and evaluation described elsewhere in this text, there are key methodological elements that should be considered in the presentation of results. These include a discussion of the context of the data; the implications of using a qualitative, quantitative, or mixed methods approach; the strengths and limitations of the study or the analysis; and the potential impact of missing data. For the more advanced student affairs professional, this may also include a discussion of the implications of the results for student affairs practice, policy, theory, or future study (*ACPA/NASPA Professional Competencies Rubric,* 2016, p. 16).

The discussion of the context for the study or the analysis should clearly state the purpose of the analysis and the related hypotheses or questions explored. The language used to describe the analysis should be chosen with care based on the intended audience. Statistical jargon is not a useful choice for audiences that are not familiar with data analysis, though it is tempting to use statistical terminology as a "gate-keeping" mechanism (to make it harder for the untrained person to understand your findings). This applies to the next section of the report as well, the description of the data collected as well as the decisions around methodological approaches. It is worth noting that you may find audiences in general tend to accept quantitative methods more readily than qualitative or mixed methods approaches. Although qualitative approaches are easier for nonresearchers to understand, that very ease may raise doubts in their minds about the validity of qualitative research. This is one more opportunity for the student affairs professional to engage in education around data literacy, and this opportunity should not be missed in the reporting and dissemination of results.

Your discussion of the strengths and limitations of both the data and your methodological choices presents another opportunity to educate your audience. The strengths tend to be easier to describe, as they are often what draw us to the particular data or analytical method(s) that we are using. Having said that, it is not only appropriate, but absolutely critical, to be candid about limitations of your data and methods as well. Data analysis about humans is by definition messy and filled with caveats, because people are complicated and multifaceted. Of particular importance are limitations related to the sample or population being considered and limitations that may be related to missing data.

Missing data is a critical element to disclose if the "missingness" is not random. Statisticians talk about "nonignorable missingness" when there is a systematic or nonrandom element that creates the missing data (Little & Rubin, 2002). It is not always easy to determine when missing data is not random, but it is important to pay attention to the possibility that patterns in missingness can teach us something important.

Consider this real-life example from a program evaluation project centered on women's cardiovascular health. A community organization dedicated to improving African-American women's cardiovascular health provided blood pressure, weight, and abdominal circumference measurements to women at local churches every few months over the course of a year; the organization also provided nutritional and health information for women to focus on between the times they were measured.[1] An analysis of the data revealed that the participants had completed the blood pressure and weight measurements in equal numbers, but there was a portion of the abdominal circumference data that were missing. When following up to determine if this was a random occurrence or if something else was happening, they found that the women were more likely to be uncomfortable with having this measurement taken because the measuring tape has to be applied directly to the skin and this meant lifting up blouses or shirts to be measured. For some women this was too embarrassing, so they chose not to participate in the measure. Not only did the researchers learn something important about ways to address this (such as providing a portable screen at church sites for this measure to improve collection rates), they could share this lesson learned with other organizations engaged in similar initiatives.

Paying attention to nonrandom missing data allows us to hear missing voices that can be critically important to the work we are trying to do. An example from recent years from survey methodology has to do with missing data around gender for both faculty and students. As part of the movement related to promoting a more inclusive definition of gender, respondents would intentionally refuse to answer a binary question about gender (where the choices are simply male or female). This is certainly nonrandom missingness in that it is a clear statement by a respondent about the assumptions inherent in a question (for example, that gender is both fixed and binary). As a result of paying attention to this missingness, survey questions about gender are starting to change in terms of the assumptions, allowing respondents to answer the reframed question in a way that respects this difference. In this sense, understanding missing data can sometimes be as valuable as understanding the data you actually collect.

The majority of the report you prepare will typically focus on your findings as well as related recommendations for follow-up action or further exploration. It is very useful for this part of the report to go back and review the scope of the analysis that you developed before you undertook your data collection to ensure that your findings address the question(s) you had set out to answer. This is not to say that you should be limited to those initial questions if your analysis

---

1. Example used with permission from the *Prime Time Sister Circles*® intervention of The Gaston & Porter Health Improvement Center, Inc.

reveals additional information that is useful to include. It is sometimes the case that in seeking to answer one set of questions, other important findings begin to emerge. This is especially true for qualitative or mixed methods projects. If this occurs, it is appropriate to include additional findings, but it is important to provide a context for how or why those findings are important in light of the original scope of the analysis. At the same time, related to the discussion of missingness above, when reporting findings, it is important to consider the reporting of nonfindings as well (recall the example above about the learning communities course pilot). If you expect to find a relationship among certain variables related to assessment or an intervention and you don't find it, the exploration of that nonfinding can be just as important as the analysis you do for data that does support your hypotheses. It is best to be transparent and honest about the fact that you didn't find a statistically significant relationship, for example, and talk about why you think that is so in relation to the data you gathered. There is a temptation here sometimes to report findings as significant by just increasing the cutoff of the value you use (which is usually .05 in the social sciences), but it is better to report your findings as they are and then provide a discussion for what other factors you think might be at work related to this outcome.

Thinking about the skill level of audiences for your report is also important when determining how to best report your findings. It is not often the case in higher education that we are presenting to audiences who are homogeneous in their abilities around data analysis, so it is useful to assume that the consumers of your report are not data experts and present your findings with that in mind. Do not assume that everyone understands standard deviation or probability statistics. A few brief sentences highlighting the main points of the charts, graphs, or data you present provide the professional context for your analysis while ensuring that your readers can understand the lens you used in your analysis. Your findings should not just be presented as a series of charts or graphs with no narrative. The narrative you provide is key to providing context for your results.

After you have presented your findings, your report will usually conclude with recommendations for follow-up action or further exploration, including a brief justification for each. In the case of assessment work, these recommendations are usually related to "closing the feedback loop," using results to refine or retool student learning goals or action steps related to the achievement of those goals. For program evaluation, recommendations are often related to refining interventions or exploring new techniques or modes of intervention (programming). Regardless of the nature of the recommendations or follow-up actions presented, it is important to provide a brief justification (linking the recommendation back to your results) to enable the reader to understand the links between your findings and what you are concluding in your recommendations.

Reporting Style

Adjusting your reporting style based on the audience(s) you are addressing is an important skill to develop. In addition to the comprehensive traditional report described above, a common format for disseminating findings is the executive summary. An executive summary is typically no longer than two or three pages and includes a brief description of each of the elements of the full report, but focuses more attention on the highlights of the findings, lessons learned, and recommendations for next steps. This is often the most challenging part of presenting findings, that is, distilling the results into a summary that is accessible, representative of the entire report, yet brief enough to be read in a few pages. An even shorter version of this is the one-page summary, which is very often what senior administrators want to see in order to get a top-level sense of the key findings and recommendations. Writing with brevity is a skill that takes practice to master. The one-page summary done well can be a powerful tool to share with multiple audiences to tell the story of your data analysis and interpretations.

Choosing a style for reporting should take into account several related elements: the type of report you need to prepare, the intended audience, the complexity of the analysis, and the method of delivery, including whether you will deliver the report in person or if it needs to stand alone as a final product. Figure 1 provides a useful conceptual framework for weighing each of these elements in your decisions about reporting. It is important to note that a single, comprehensive, traditional report might generate numerous smaller reports, based on your considerations of each of the elements as shown in Figure 6.1.

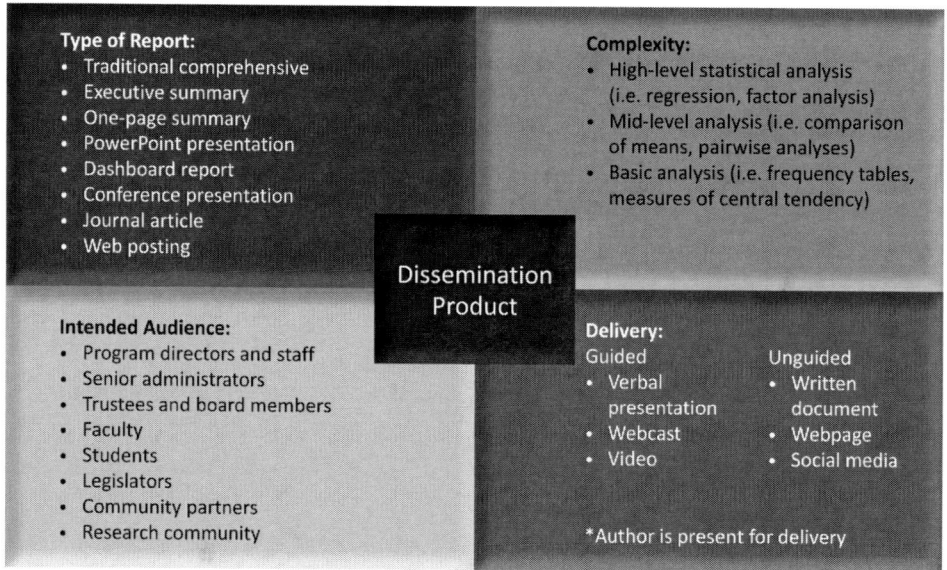

Figure 6.1[2]. Dissemination Product Matrix.

In this context, a written executive summary focused on midlevel analysis for a group of senior administrators would become the dissemination product. These elements can be combined in any number of ways to create your dissemination product, though it is certainly the case that some elements make more sense to pair together than others. For example, it would not be very useful to prepare a high-level statistical analysis and try to deliver it via social media or to present a journal article to a council of trustees. But considering each of these components in the creation of your dissemination product can be a useful reminder to balance the elements of complexity, intended audience, report type, and delivery method (guided or unguided).

Using Findings: Demonstrating Outcomes and Advocacy

The ultimate goal of any data report is typically to inform next steps in the decision-making process with which stakeholders must engage in order to continue to work towards institutional goals. As noted above, a key component of this process is using findings to

---

2. This chart is based upon the work of the Centers for Disease Control and Prevention, 2013, *Evaluating Reporting: A guide to help ensure use of evaluation findings*, pp. 9–10.

demonstrate program impacts and the achievement of goals through the presentation of data in appropriate modalities and venues. The next step, of course, is to make decisions about program continuation or refinement based on the recommendations related to the results of the data analysis. Chapter 4 described how to develop outcome goals using the SMART technique, and this same technique can be applied to using results to translate recommendations into goals and develop related actions. It is important to note here that setting realistic and achievable goals based on relevant data is key to making informed decisions.

Retention data are a good example to consider here. Let us suppose that you are working with partners in academic affairs around retention of first-year students and you are collaborating on wrap-around programming for a first-year experience to increase students' sense of belonging. While you may be able to demonstrate that retention from fall to fall (first-year to second-year fall) has increased, care should be taken in goal setting around both the magnitude and speed with which greater increases can be expected. This is because retention in and of itself is a multifaceted phenomenon. In most cases it would be unrealistic to expect retention to be above a certain "leveling-out" percentage that reflects the ebb and flow of factors unrelated to students' sense of belonging. For example, if retention is 78% in the first year of the program, and you set a goal to increase retention by 5% each year for the next four years (to 98%), it is unlikely that the goal will be met due to the expected movement of students in and out of the university even under conditions where all students feel a high degree of belonging.

Building a culture of assessment and a culture of data-informed decision making has been a goal of numerous institutions in the last two decades. This means that most student affairs professionals will find it necessary to use data and results when advocating for new resources or the reallocation of existing resources. In this context, it is critical to understand the culture of your institution when choosing how to present your findings and how to best position your program or division when advocating for resources. One of the most common mistakes in these efforts is confusing outputs (the activities or services provided) with outcomes (the results or impact achieved).

Consider again the example of the after-hours programming for first-year residential students in order to increase their feelings of belonging. Let us say that you demonstrate increased numbers of students attending at least 50% of the sessions from 60% to 70% in one year, and based on this outcome you are looking to increase funding for the program in order to expand it to a broader student population. Using the chart in Figure 6.1, you determine that a one-page summary of the programming and a graph illustrating this significant increase in participation is the best method for presenting your request to the university's budget review committee. At the committee meeting, you share your one-page report, proudly demonstrating the increase in students participating and someone asks, "So what?" Of course, the point of your program wasn't just to get students to attend, it was to increase their feeling of belonging. By focusing only on the increase in participation (the output), you would have missed focusing on the positive change in students' feelings of belonging (the outcome). Numbers of participants are important to note, but not as a sole data point. They are meaningless without some metric related to the impact of the participation on the students involved.

It is worth noting that while we need to advocate for our programs and our division, we also have a professional responsibility to disseminate results in ways that take into account the strengths and limitations of implications for practice, policy, theory, or future study (*ACPA/NASPA Professional Competencies Rubrics,* 2016, p. 16). This requires a commitment to the elements discussed at the beginning of this chapter related to accuracy and transparency in reporting, as well as a commitment to sharing both findings and nonfindings. Good research practice is a discipline. It is critical to remember that you cannot lose that discipline as you advocate at your institution to secure funding and support for the work you are doing with students.

Collaboration: The Key to Sustainable Improvement

As Kennedy-Phillips and Ross described in Chapter 3, the interpretation of data and sharing results has political implications. It is critical to understand institutional culture in this context, but there is another political element that is important as well: agenda setting. It is a well-known maxim of political science that agenda-setting is the key to advancing policy initiatives (Kingdon, 2010). In this context, being able to identify a problem or challenge, as well as the solution, are necessary but insufficient conditions for change: the political opportunity to change is also a requirement, and this is what it takes to get issues onto an agenda. Those of us working in institutions of higher education can benefit greatly from understanding this principle in the ways in which we seek to promote student success through defining problems and offering solutions.

It can be very frustrating to know you have identified a barrier to student success, to know you have good evidence around a sound solution to addressing the problem, but to feel like you are getting nowhere at your institution in terms of getting anyone's attention or getting a critical mass of other colleagues to support your efforts. When you find yourself in this situation, it is likely because the issue is not a priority on the institution's agenda or your division's agenda. So how do you get the initiatives that you are working for onto the institutional or divisional agenda?

What Kingdon refers to as the "policy window" is applicable to the work we do in higher education. Kingdon contends that there are three streams that develop independently of each other and are often unrelated: the problem stream (issues that require attention), the policy stream (proposals for change, solutions that are known), and the politics stream (the political conditions of your institution in this case). When there is a confluence of these three streams—when a problem is recognized, when a solution is available, and the political climate is conducive to change—a policy window (or a window of opportunity) opens which can facilitate change (Guldbrandsson & Fossum, 2009). Referring to a lobbyist he interviewed for his seminal work, Kingdon states, "In the process he talks about windows, he talks about the importance of advocates being ready to move when the window opens, he talks about their inability to create forces that prompt change, and he talks about their ability to take advantage of such forces when they come along" (Kingdon, 2001, p. 337). Kingdon adds, quoting the lobbyist himself, "When you lobby for something, what you have to do is put together your coalition. You have to gear up. You have to get your political forces in line and then you sit there and wait for the fortuitous event. . . . As I see it, people who are trying to advocate change are like surfers waiting for the big wave. You get out there, you have to be ready to go, you have to be ready to paddle. If you are not ready to paddle when the big wave comes along, you are not going to ride it in" (Kingdon, 2001 p. 337). The lesson here for the student affairs professional advocating for change is that it is critical to be prepared with sound results and data-informed recommendations, ready to act, to ride the wave, when the institutional opportunity presents itself.

A real-life example of this builds on Kingdon's work by linking it to another key element, that of framing findings and recommendations in contexts outside of the institution, such as national or regional conversations. In recent years, many institutions have struggled with issues of sexual violence and the challenge of training faculty, staff, and students around this critical issue. Sexual violence is not new, nor are the best practices around preventing it and providing support for those who are the victims of such violence. Yet, gaining traction on training and intervention has been challenging for many institutions. Student affairs professionals working in this area, however, remained focused on developing training and improving support for those who experience sexual violence. And in the wake of national conversations and crises on campuses around the country regarding sexual violence, there is urgency around moving the needle on this issue on campuses that student affairs professionals can leverage to align the "streams" around this issue. As a result, well-prepared student affairs professionals at campuses across the county are now able to "ride the wave" of this policy window to make lasting and significant changes on their campuses.

Implicit in this approach, of course, is an understanding of who the stakeholders are when using results to make decisions to align resources. Making results meaningful across divisions means understanding the perspectives of multiple stakeholders. While it is easy to remember to include program staff, directors, faculty, and administrators as stakeholders in this sort of work, it is important to remember that students are stakeholders as well. This means that they have a role beyond being the subjects of much of the analysis we undertake. It is critically important to provide mechanisms for student representation amongst the stakeholders to which you provide data and recommendations to ensure that their voices are not lost in the analysis. The simplest way to do this is to develop a practice of ensuring student seats on the committees that review data analyses and make recommendations about both actions and funding commitments for those commitments. This has the added appeal to the student affairs professional of providing a significant professional development opportunity for students in a cocurricular experience.

A further key to success as a collaborative colleague is both understanding the importance of giving stakeholders a "heads up" about
your findings before you present them and understanding the culture
of shared governance at your institution. Even if your findings are
"good" and you think they will make stakeholders happy, it is important to provide an opportunity for those with whom you are trying to
build relationships to give them a sense of the findings before they
hear them in public for the first time or read about them in a final
published report or document. This is not to say that you should
adjust your findings based on their feedback, but you may find that
they have helpful advice about how to adjust your message or set the
context for what you wish to share. Sometimes this messaging is related to the culture of shared governance at your institution. For example, do the faculty feel like the development and assessment of student
learning outcomes about critical thinking are solely the domain of curricular instruction? If so, you may want to frame your student learning outcomes around this skill in a way that links critical thinking to
both curricular and cocurricular experiences rather than talking about
them only in terms of the cocurricular experience. This way, your
findings can be heard rather than launching a battle between who
"owns" critical thinking at the institution.

In the case where your findings will be difficult for stakeholders (or
other audiences in general) to accept, even more care is required.
Again, the results are the results and your findings and related recommendations should be transparent and based on the data you have
analyzed. However, the timing and process related to your dissemination of the findings should reflect a commitment to a disposition to
collaborate, as noted in the ACPA/NASPA competencies. Providing
stakeholders with a preview of what you are going to share allows
them to prepare a response (should they need one) in advance and to
think through the ways they want to message the findings, especially
if your findings are challenging for them to address.

As noted above, collaboration across divisions at an institution
tends to make outcomes better because when it comes to honing and
refining your ideas, there is nothing like trying to convince someone
from a different area that your approach is as good as or better than
the existing approach. There is even a more practical benefit as well:
in an era of scarce resources and competing priorities, collaboration

is essential to both getting and maintaining institutional support for the initiatives you undertake. Student affairs professionals must achieve a balance between advocacy for divisional needs and a commitment to the financial well-being of the institution as a whole.

A practical "win-win" approach can be very useful in achieving this goal. For example, while it is always less complicated to hire full-time permanent people to provide programming for students, in some cases a collaborative approach that might garner support from those in academic affairs at universities that have graduate programs would be to consider using graduate assistants (GAs) to provide staffing for some entry-level work around student programming (i.e., interfacing with students under the supervision of a director for student leadership initiatives). For the student affairs professional, the workload is greater because you will have to train new people on a regular basis (as GAs complete their degrees). However, if you can make use of GAs to do programming work, the graduate dean, college deans, and provost may become advocates of your program simply because they can provide more financial aid to graduate students this way. In addition, if the graduate programs at your institution require professional service as part of training, you can leverage that for your programming as well. In this sense, while working to reduce costs you can build partnerships that are sustainable and will have the effect of prioritizing your programming.

Another area where this can be achieved is related to assessment and evaluation. These skills are now clearly part of the ACPA/NASPA expected competencies for student affairs professionals, yet these are areas that also consume a lot of time and effort for those in academic affairs. Partnerships between student affairs and academic affairs on the assessment and evaluation and general education outcomes, for example, both inside and outside the curriculum, are a key area where collaborations can both produce better results and promote student success while reducing institutional costs. Also, the assessment and evaluation of service learning, community engagement, and leadership experiences are areas where natural partnerships may emerge since many universities include these elements in both the curricular and co-curricular experiences for students.

Case Study and Self-assessment

This chapter has focused on the following key elements:

- Interpreting data in practical terms that are relevant to your institutional context.
- Presenting results accurately and fairly in reports that are useful to a variety of audiences.
- Using findings to make informed decisions and to align resources.
- Understanding the importance of collaboration with stakeholders and windows of opportunity for advancing the work of student affairs professionals around student learning and student success.
- Understanding agenda-setting and how to leverage policy windows to make significant change.

The following case study provides an opportunity to apply these skills and to assess your response in light of these competencies.

Case Study

You are part of a work group cochaired by a Student Affairs director and the Associate Provost for Student Success from the division of Academic Affairs. The work group has been charged by the President to gather information around the prevalence of alcohol use by undergraduate students and potential links to their retention and academic performance. The President is asking for a joint report from Student Affairs and Academic Affairs to share at an upcoming Council of Trustees meeting to both provide information on the issue and to propose next steps to address this issue. The President also wants your team to distribute reports to Student Affairs and Academic Affairs leaders so they can begin to address this issue. Your team, which includes people with expertise in survey development and data analysis, deploys a survey that yields a good return rate that is sufficiently representative of the undergraduate student body.

Your team completes the analysis of the data and is now preparing the report for the Council of Trustees. Your team has decided to focus on the following key findings for the report:

- Students who reported using alcohol one or more times per week had lower GPAs (to a statistically significant degree) than those who reported that they do not use alcohol.
- Students who reported using alcohol one or more times per week had significantly lower retention rates than those who reported they do not use alcohol.
- Alcohol use appears to be more prevalent among students who are involved in Greek life.
- Male respondents reported engaging in binge drinking at a higher rate than female respondents.

Your team also notes the following about the data generated from the survey:

- Female respondents were more likely to skip questions about binge drinking than male respondents, so there is a portion of data missing for this set of questions for female students.

Questions for Consideration

1. Given the findings the team has decided to focus on, what are the primary elements of interpretation of the data to which you should pay attention in preparing the reports? Think about data definitions, missing data, understanding the relationship between causality and correlation, and avoiding bias in the interpretation of results.

2. What style of report, level of complexity, and delivery method makes the most sense for the Council of Trustees? What would make sense for the other audiences in the divisions of Student Affairs and Academic Affairs?

3. What elements of collaboration may be important to the report that you are preparing? What "policy window" implications are there for this report and subsequent action steps?

Self-assessment

Using your response to the case above, answer the following questions:

1. What issues related to data definitions, missing data, and avoiding bias were part of the considerations you need to take into account for this case?

2. How did your response take into account the audience(s) to whom you are presenting your findings? Did that factor into your decisions around the content and the style of your report?

3. Were you able to strategize a plan for successful collaboration around next steps? Did you link the policy window opportunities to the external (national) dialogue about undergraduate alcohol use?

Reflections on the Case

1. *Given the findings the team has decided to focus on, what are the primary elements of interpretation of the data to which you should pay attention in preparing the reports? Think about data definitions, missing data, understanding the relationship between causality and correlation, and avoiding bias in the interpretation of results.* There are several key areas to pay attention to when interpreting and reporting on these findings. The link between alcohol use and lower academic performance as measured by GPA is a well-established one, yet this does not imply causality. It is tempting to assume a causal relationship, so it is important to make sure in the report that other factors that are also highly correlated with GPA are taken into account. For example, high school class rank and high school GPA are highly correlated with university GPA. In addition, apparent GPA variances that disappear when controlling for courses with known high rates of failure (such as particular general education courses), should be taken into account. The same considerations apply to the findings regarding reten-

tion. It would be important to take into account student engagement as measured by participation in cocurricular programs, for example, when interpreting these findings since engagement is highly correlated with retention. In this sense, it may be the case that students who report using alcohol are also the students who are not engaged, and alcohol use alone does not explain their lack of retention. It is also important here to avoid bias about cocurricular programs that have been linked to alcohol use. Participation in Greek life has been linked to increased alcohol use, but it important to apply the same care to the interpretation of this finding even though it would seem to confirm some stereotypes about Greek life on college campuses. For example, national data tell us that commuter students have the lowest incidence of alcohol use. At the same time, residential students tend to be the most active in Greek life. One should consider the effect of residential/commuter status on this finding and include that as part of the discussion. Data definitions are also a key part of this analysis and should be addressed in the reports. How is alcohol use defined? How is binge drinking defined? How is retention defined? GPA is the only term used in the findings that has a straightforward meaning, and in that sense, it is important to provide data definitions for all the terms that are multidimensional. Finally, there is a clear instance of missing data in these findings and it does seem to qualify as nonrandom missingness. Why might female respondents skip questions about binge drinking? And what impact does this have on the finding that male respondents reported higher rates of binge drinking?

2. *What style of report, level of complexity, and delivery method makes the most sense for the Council of Trustees? What would make sense for the other audiences in the divisions of Student Affairs and Academic Affairs?* The dissemination product matrix in Figure 6.1 of this chapter is a useful tool for determining the types or reports the work group should generate. For the Council of Trustees, a guided presentation including a PowerPoint and a one-page summary is a good choice. You could also supplement this with an executive summary, which would provide a nonguided piece for the group to refer to after your presentation. For the divisions of Student Affairs and Academic Affairs, the same pieces could be shared, but you would most likely want to prepare a traditional

comprehensive report since these groups will want a much deeper analysis and they will need this level of detail to develop an action plan or steps to address the issue as charged by the President.

3. *What elements of collaboration may be important to the report that you are preparing? What "policy window" implications are there for this report and subsequent action steps?* It is clear that the President expects collaboration between Student Affairs and Academic Affairs in both assessing this issue and developing an action plan or next steps. It is important for you and your team to be aware of likely areas of "finger-pointing" (assigning blame) based on the findings you will share and focus on collaboration throughout the process in anticipation of these issues. For example, faculty might find it easy to blame Greek life participation on alcohol use, and therefore see no role for Academic Affairs to play in addressing this issue. Your team, however, will likely talk about how student engagement broadly defined is a countervailing force to alcohol use and in this sense, it may the case that faculty themselves will be asked to help students feel more engaged as part of the action steps the work group recommends. The policy window implications for this issue are significant and as a student affairs professional, it would be important for you to contribute your knowledge of the national conversation on this issue to the work group. For example, the National Institute on Alcohol Abuse and Alcoholism (part of the National Institutes of Health) is an excellent resource for data as well as for strategies for prevention of college drinking (www.niaaa.nih.gov).

The next chapter will continue to build upon the concept of assessment, evaluation, and research by expanding on AER's relevancy with regards to creating a greater sense of transparency and accountability. It is important that student affairs professionals be prepared to plan and execute quality, outcome-based programs and services. To ensure that this occurs, student affairs professionals must commit to AER as a major component of our development and our professional identity. This commitment will transform how we go about contributing to the academy and completing the educational mission of any college or university.

Chapter 7

THE ROLE OF ASSESSMENT, EVALUATION, AND RESEARCH IN PROFESSIONAL DEVELOPMENT AND PROFESSIONAL IDENTITY

JENNIFER MASSEY AND KYLE D. MASSEY

Using Assessment, Evaluation, and Research for Professional Development and Professional Identity

As indicated in previous chapters in this book, assessment, evaluation, and research (AER) skills and practices in student affairs are essential at multiple levels: within programs, across divisions, across institutions, and nationally and internationally. This importance is reinforced by calls for greater transparency and accountability in higher education. Ensuring student affairs professionals are trained in AER practice and given the opportunity to use these skills in their work is a pressing priority for the field.

Planning and executing programs that engage students, build community on campus, and enrich the student experience are essential components of many student affairs roles. To achieve excellence in this, and every other aspect of student affairs work, professionals must commit to AER as major components of their work; assessment must become a state of mind that informs daily routine (Henning & Roberts, 2016). This intentional approach will transform the daily operations of student affairs professionals and position the discipline of student affairs an essential component to the overall educational mission of any college or university. Utilizing research, being reflective, incorporating data for informed decision making when appropriate, and assessing the impact of the programs and services emanating from divisions of student affairs further supports the relevance of this work to the academy. AER should be central elements of the culture of all student affairs departments (Bresciani, Moore-Gardner, & Hickmott, 2009; Ryder & Kimball, 2015) and core to student affairs professional identity (Sriram & Oster, 2012).

The concept of professional identity is closely tied to one's sense of self in both professional and personal capacities. Professional identity in student affairs develops over time through a process, or multiple processes, of socialization, and involves gaining insight into professional practices and the development of the skills and values of the field (Massey, 2017). Assessment, evaluation, and research have significant roles to play in the professional identity and career development of student affairs professionals, and have been identified by professional associations as one of the core competency areas for student affairs in the United Sates (ACPA & NASPA, 2015) and Canada (Fernandez, Fitzgerald, Hambler, & Mason-Innes, 2016). Career development theory and research have emphasized the centrality of identity to one's development as a professional. Holland (1997) states that professional identity signifies someone possessing a clear picture of their own goals, interests, and talents, and which provides people with a vision of their career plans, their contingency plans, and their ability to implement these plans. Using this as a premise for this chapter, it can be said that as an emerging or new practitioner, your professional identity is intrinsically linked to your professional development. Therefore, keeping AER central in one's professional identity can serve as a guide for continued development as a student affairs professional (Bettencourt, Malaney, Kidder, & George Mwangi, 2017).

Do not lose sight of the importance of this competency area after graduation and as your career progresses. This chapter exhorts all student affairs professionals to keep AER central to their conception of self as scholar-practitioners, and to use AER to inform ongoing professional development.

This chapter will focus on four main areas. First is the importance of AER for individual professional identity. We will outline the role of AER in cultivating a professional expertise, which can then be leveraged for one's career development and the construction of an individual professional identity. Second, we will discuss how assessment, evaluation, and research are essential for strategic planning at the divisional scale. Next, we will explain the value and utility that assessment, evaluation, and research have in articulating the role of student affairs on campus, which includes elucidating the impact the work of student affairs professionals have on student learning and engagement. Finally, will we discuss the role of AER in shaping national and international conversations about the field. We anticipate that as an increasing number of student affairs professionals reimagine their role as scholar-practitioners, there will be a broader conversation about the changing priorities, frames of reference, best practices, and standards within the professional (Shutt, Garrett, Lynch, & Dean, 2012).

AER's Role in Individual Professional Identity

Recognized as one of the core competency areas for student affairs, AER plays an important role in fostering individual professional identity. Professional identity in student affairs is defined individually by what it means to be a student affairs professional, including a personal philosophy of education, a commitment to a certain set of professional ethics and values, an understanding and interpretation of the numerous theories that underpin the profession, and acquired skills cultivated through one's experiences in the field. AER as a competency is crucial for deepening your philosophical and theoretical proficiency, and cultivating excellence in applying theory to practice (Banta, 2002). Routinely embedding AER into practice facilitates an ongoing continuous improvement processes within your department, which cultivates excellence in student affairs practice. In this way, AER is core to professional development because it nurtures an expertise that can support career advancement, which will enable one to highlight the distinctive knowledge, skills, and competencies acquired over time in the field (Erwin & Wise, 2002). Collectively, these practices will deepen and enrich your own conception of your professional identity as a student affairs professional.

Reciprocal Relationship in Student Affairs Theory and Practice

Assessment, evaluation, and research are core to the scholar-practitioner approach that defines student affairs professional practice (Sriram, 2011). All student affairs professionals should ascribe to the scholar-practitioner approach, which allows individuals to move seamlessly between theory and practice (Ryder & Kimball, 2015). Scholar-practitioners adopt AER as a reflexive process, which enables them to draw from theory, apply and adapt theory to the local context, explore the extent to which the theory accurately accounts for specific contexts, and, through engaging in conference presentations and publishing, provide feedback to further inform and nuance the theories underpinning professional practice.

At Baylor University in Texas, for example, the New Student Programs office intentionally applied theory to its implementation and assessment of orientation student leader training (Massey, Sulak, & Sriram, 2013). The staff who make up this dynamic and student-centered team of student affairs professionals developed learning outcomes for orientation leader training based upon the concept of servant leadership, a philosophy of leading that embraces service to others (Keith, 2008). More specifically, orientation leaders were expected to engage new students in the core values of Baylor University's new student experience program—connection, identity, reflection, friendship, and tradition (Massey et al., 2013). The New Student Programs office applied Kolb's (1984) model of experiential learning to the design and delivery of training to provide intentional opportunities for orientation leaders to gain the required learning outcomes. Training for all orientation leaders began at the conception stage of Kolb's cycle, with all student leaders required to register and pass a leadership development course prior to their summer leadership experience. The course explored the theory of servant leadership and students were taught behaviors and values associated with this approach. After successfully completing the course, students served as leaders during an extended summer orientation program (Massey et al., 2013).

Staff involved in the program at Baylor measured student learning throughout the various stages of the learning experience to explore the extent to which each required classroom and experiential component of the training impacted the knowledge, skills, and abilities of upper-year student leaders. They found student learning increased significantly during the classroom portion of the training program, but stagnated during the experiential component. Upon careful review of the experiential component, it was identified that opportunities were limited for student leaders to engage in structured reflection during the experiential component of the learning experience. Recognizing reflection as a crucial element of the theory underpinning experiential learning, the New Student Programs staff concluded this was a key reason why student leaders had not advanced in their knowledge, skills, and abilities during the experiential component of the learning experience. The New Student Programs office subsequently revised the training program to include more structured and frequent opportunities for student leaders to reflect on their learning. In addition, some of those involved published and presented their findings to further inform theory development and its application to practice (Massey et al., 2013). This reciprocal relationship between theory and practice is an important element of the profession. By integrating AER into daily practice, student affairs professionals enrich their philosophical and theoretical proficiency and ensure their work is theoretically informed (Reason & Kimball, 2012).

Cultivating Professional Excellence

Student affairs professionals who consistently integrate AER into their workflow refine their knowledge and skills and advance their professional expertise. Bettencourt et al. (2017) note that "finding better ways to interweave theory and context may not only lead to better implementation in the field, but a higher caliber of professionals" (p. 97). In their book *A Guide to Becoming a Scholarly Practitioner in Student Affairs,* Hatfield and Wise (2015) highlight the importance of practitioners engaging in scholarship and offer practical advice to student affairs professionals who want to adopt a scholar-practitioner approach. While professional development is often conceived/defined as narrowly as traveling to professional conferences (which is often one of the first things cut from budgets during times of fiscal constraints), engaging in AER is a part of a broader strategy to manage one's continuous learning and professional development. By integrating AER into your regular workflow, you are empowered to critically engage in assessing what works and what does not This supports the asking and answering of important questions about why a program, resource, or support may or may not be offering optimal benefits to students. Embracing AER in this reflexive way facilitates the interplay between theory and practice.

While the scholar-practitioner approach is cited broadly as best practice for student affairs, it is also widely recognized that professionals in the field encounter many obstacles when trying to stay current in the literature of student affairs (Schroeder & Pike, 2001). Four key barriers observed by Sriram (2011) hinder many student affairs professionals in their efforts to realize a scholar-practitioner approach: inadequate preparation, tyranny of the urgent, lack of clear purpose, and cultural discouragement. Inadequate preparation could be as a consequence of a graduate program that did not emphasize research and scholarship or because the program was completed a long time ago, which leads to staff feeling underprepared to engage with scholarship. Tyranny of the urgent, in which the nature of many student affairs roles requires quick responses to pressing situations on campus, is exasperated by the growing workload many student affairs professionals report. A lack of clear purpose arises when student affairs leaders do not adequately connect what is happening in the day-to-day with trends in the literature, so their staff struggle to see the point of making time for scholarship. Cultural discouragement is often implicit in student affairs departments where few people are actively and visibly engaged in scholarship, and where leadership does not support, reinforce, or recognize scholarly pursuit. Hatfield and Wise (2015) identified similar challenges encountered by student affairs professionals seeking to adopt a scholar-practitioner approach, such as low motivation of, limited expectations by, time constraints of, and lack of support from supervisors as key roadblocks.

To address the obstacles many student affairs professionals identify when trying to integrate scholarship and practice, Sriram (2011) encourages professionals to make an active commitment to lifelong learning so they hone and advance their skills throughout their career. He suggests practitioners take the first 15 minutes of every day to read, thereby embedding scholarship into their daily routine; engage in topical research, identifying opportunities to connect reading to practice; and establish a reading group to promote a culture of scholarship. Kezar (2000) agrees: "the solution for dissolving a socially constructed false dichotomy is to create a new culture, socializing the field to a philosophy that emphasizes continuity and mutuality" (p. 464). Situating AER as central to and not disconnected from professional practice will advance the professional identity and development of student affairs professionals.

Advancing Career Development

For new professionals entering the field, integrating assessment, evaluation, and research into the routine of their professional practice offers an opportunity to distinguish themselves within the profession and advance their career. Given it is widely accepted that the scholar-practitioner is the preferred approach to student affairs practice and noting that relatively few student affairs professionals manage to balance scholarship and administration, senior student affairs officers are often impressed with candidates who demonstrate their commitment to AER during a hiring process (Sriram & Oster, 2012; Bettencourt et al., 2017). Student affairs professionals who normalize AER as a central component to their work can leverage this to differentiate themselves and advance their career development opportunities. Sriram (2011) observes that student affairs professionals who successfully balance scholarship and practice are "role models in the field" (p. 1). Intentionally fostering AER as part of routine professional practice early in one's career facilitates professional networking. This can have an impact on career opportunities, help to foster a national reputation as an expert, and provide a platform to connect with, influence, and emerge as a national thought leader.

Presenting AER activities at conferences, for example, provides opportunities for professional networking between sessions and at the social events that typically start and end the day. Colleagues from different universities often establish connections when they watch an engaging conference presentation that is grounded in AER. Likewise, scholar-practitioners can foster a national reputation for excellence by regularly contributing to the published literature on student affairs, and assessment projects often provide rich data upon which articles and reports can be written.

Deepen Professional Identity

Approaching AER as a reflexive practice enhances the professional identity of student affairs professionals (Baxter Magolda & Magolda, 2011). Ryder and Kimball (2015) argue "reflexivity promotes mindfulness and intentionality through sustained attention to how student affairs professionals' values, beliefs, and assumptions influence practice" (p. 34). Thus, AER as a reflexive practice requires student affairs professionals to be conscious of the reciprocal relationship between attitudes, philosophy, knowledges, and their practice, which are all core components of their professional identity.

Using AER to Cultivate a Professional Identity for Student Affairs Division

Assessment, evaluation, and research are not only important to advancing individual professional identity, professional development planning, and career advancement; they also play a fundamental role in shaping and articulating the professional identity of the field of student affairs on campus. They are paramount to the establishment and implementation of a division of student affairs strategic plan, which operationalizes a shared professional identity (Clark & Brown, 2017; Henning & Roberts, 2016). Research guides the philosophy of professional practice within a division of student affairs (Evans, Forney, Guido, Patton, & Renn, 2010; Hamrick, Evans, & Schuh, 2002). The assessment process empowers all staff working in student affairs to determine, describe, and document the distinctive impact of their work on student learning (Schuh, Biddix, Dean, & Kinzie, 2016; Yousey-Elsner, Bentrin, & Henning, 2015). Evaluation guides continuous improvement for co-curricular learning, informing strategic decisions about areas for improvement and future investment, and provides opportunities to highlight the distinctive expertise of student affairs staff (Henning & Roberts, 2016; Schuh & Upcraft, 1998; Suskie, 2018). Collectively, assessment, evaluation, and research enable senior student affairs officers to sculpt a unique professional identity for the division. Situating the work of student affairs within a framework that clearly identifies learning outcomes and sound assessment processes facilitates strategic alignment and collaboration with academic colleagues across the institution to achieve shared goals.

AER to Guide Strategic Alignment and Continuous Improvement

Situating the work of student affairs within a framework that clearly identifies learning outcomes and sound assessment practices will facilitate strategic alignment and collaboration across the division and across the institution around shared goals. Assessment, evaluation, and research play a fundamental role in shaping and articulating the professional identity of student affairs on campus. AER is central to the strategic planning process within student affairs, a key outcome of which is the creation, revision, or affirmation of the mission and vision of the division. Strategic planning offers an opportunity for a division of student affairs to assert its collective commitment to the development of student-centered, learning-focused cocurricular programing. Through this process, senior leadership, in consultation with staff and students, define what the division hopes to accomplish through the programs and supports offered to students (Banta & Palomba, 2014).

Embedding AER into the strategic planning process involves answering a key question: *How are we empowering all students to succeed?* Ensuring the strategic plan is grounded in contemporary literature is essential. Before we can define how we are empowering all students to succeed we need to know what constitutes success and the factors that support or impede student success. Thus, theoretically informed practice is fundamental to the work of student affairs. Staying current with, and ideally contributing to, the literature on higher education and student affairs helps ensure the programs, supports, and resources that are provided will enhance student success and reflect best practice in the field (Shutt et al., 2012).

Accreditation processes and demands from governmental agencies and other external bodies have encouraged postsecondary institutions to pay closer attention to assessing their impact in advancing the knowledge and skills of students (Bresciani et al., 2009; Ryder & Kimball, 2015). While these processes play out differently in various jurisdictions and regions across the United States and Canada, the overall impact of these demands and pressures is that institutions ask for more and more data from their various academic departments to demonstrate continuous improvement of learning. In student affairs, there remains much work to fully integrate assessment of student learning in the cocurricular context into regular practice (Bowman, 2013). When student affairs divisions do this well, they are able to demonstrate the impact of their work, which helps to legitimize institutional investment in student affairs (Culp, 2012).

National and International

AER will continue to shape national and international conversations about the field as more student affairs professionals redefine their role as scholar-practitioners, conversations about the priorities of the field, frames of reference, best practices, and standards within the profession (Shutt et al., 2012). In Canada, for example, there is a growing focus on decolonization and Indigenization of the academy. Student affairs is at the forefront of much of this work, informed by existing AER practices and by approaching assessment through other ways of knowing. The Awareness Project, housed in the Department of Geography at Queen's University, is working with student affairs divisions across the country to critically examine what students at Canadian universities know (and importantly don't know) about Indigenous peoples in Canada (e.g., Godlewska, Massey, Adjei, & Moore, 2013; Godlewska, Schaefli, Massey, Freake, Adjei, Rose, & Hudson, 2017). The findings of this work are informing the (re)development of curricular and cocurricular programing at universities across the country as Canadian postsecondary education strives to respond to the calls to action in the final report by the Truth and Reconciliation Commission of Canada (2015).

As student affairs professionals continue to grapple with how to advance student success and empower all students to thrive, AER will become increasingly more important. Equity and social justice are foundational principles of a student affairs identity and are important lenses through which student affairs professionals are engaging progressively in AER. To expand critical understandings of the structures that support and impede different groups of students requires critical engagement with AER in which the voices and experiences of those underrepresented in higher education are advanced. AER enables student affairs professionals to identify and challenge institutional and societal forces that create differential education opportunities and experiences for students based on a range of social identities including race, gender, class, sexuality, and disability. With an increasing number of student affairs professionals recognizing their role as scholar-practitioners, national and international dialogue about how the profession identifies and responds to priorities will evolve. For new professionals entering the field, it would be wise to situate yourself within this discussion so you can help shape how standards, best practices, accreditation, and accountability are defined and addressed.

Reflection Exercises

Defining Your Personal Philosophy of Education

As a student affairs professional, you will play an important role in student learning and engagement. Approaching your work as an educator will transform how you think about, design, and execute the programs, resources, and supports you provide to students. Writing your philosophy of education is important because it helps you synthesize how you think about your work, the impact you want to make on student learning, and how you strive to make this impact. Student affairs professionals make a significant impact on student learning. Every day, student affairs professionals make decisions about what they teach students and how they teach it. These decisions are rooted in student affairs professionals' personal philosophy of education and reflect their professional identity.

Getting Started

1. Think back to your time as an undergraduate student. Describe two to three times you were most engaged on campus. **What** did those experiences involve? Identify some specific factors that enhanced your engagement. How did this level of engagement shape your learning?

2. **Why** did you decide to become a student affairs professional? Identify at least one specific area in which you want to make a difference in the lives of students. For example, *I want students to find balance in their lives and foster excellent wellness practices, or I want students to graduate as engaged civic leaders with a commitment to making a difference in their communities, or I want to enhance the cross-cultural competencies of students to empower them as agents for equity and social justice.* This is an important question because it speaks to your motivation as a student affairs professional. It situates the **"why"** at the heart of your work (Sinek, 2011) and motivation is intimately tied to professional identity.

3. **How** do/will you intentionally thread your "why" throughout your work as a student affairs professional? Think about specific ways in which your "why" informs **how** you approach your work, **how** you design experiences for students, and which activities and reflection exercises you select, etc.

---

continued

4. Finally think about **how** you design the experiences you offer as a student affairs professional. **How** do you craft opportunities for students to engage in activities that enable them to learn the content at the heart of your "why"? What pedagogical practices do those experiences entail? Can you identify how your answers to questions one and two inform your approach to supporting student learning? This is an essential step in linking theory to practice, cultivating your own professional identity, and ensuring your assessment activities are tied to student learning (Haave, 2014).

Writing Your Personal Philosophy of Education

In a couple of paragraphs summarize your reflections to the questions above in the form of a written philosophy of education statement. There are many different ways to write a philosophy of education. Feel free to use an approach that works for you. If you wish, you can use the following framework to help craft your first draft:

- As a student affairs professional I want to shape student learning by . . . (think about the "**why**" and refer to your answers to question 2 above).

- In the programs, experiences, resources, and supports to oversee I will . . . (think about **what** you will do and refer to your answer to question 1 above).

- As an important member of the postsecondary learning environment I will . . . (think about how you will achieve your goals, the specific teaching and learning strategies you will use and refer to your answers to questions 3 and 4 above).

- Assessment will be integrated into my practice by (consider how you will link your why, what, and how using assessment to advance student learning and engagement).

As a student affairs professional it is important for you to endeavor to keep assessment, evaluation, and research central to your professional identity. Collectively, assessment, evaluation, and research are important tools to help you guide and manage your ongoing professional development. At the individual level, AER will help you cultivate a professional expertise, which you can use to advance your career development. At the departmental or divisional level, AER is key to strategic planning, enabling the department to highlight its impact on student learning and engagement. When student affairs divisions intentionally embed AER into the organizational culture, the competency of the staff increase and the quality of the programs, resources, and supports they offer is enhanced. The next phase of professional development and continued scholarly development is to translate your findings into publications. Chapter 8 will fully describe the need for and benefits of the scholarship of assessment in student affairs as key to developing professional identity.

Chapter 8

THE SCHOLARSHIP OF ASSESSMENT, EVALUATION, AND RESEARCH IN STUDENT AFFAIRS

Vicki L. Wise and Lisa J. Hatfield

Why Engage in AER Scholarship?

By now, from your review of this textbook, we know you understand conceptually the similarities and differences among assessment, evaluation, and research (AER). The lines between these are often blurred in practice, however, because they all share four common elements:

- Attention to the values, ethics, and politics associated with data collection, management, analysis, and reporting.
- Well-thought-out (and critically examined) design based on a theoretical framework that aligns with organizational outcomes, goals, and values.
- Use of appropriate methodology, data collection, and data analysis given the purpose, guiding questions, and inferences.
- Appropriate interpretation, reporting, and use of results relevant to the institutional context, the varied stakeholder interests, and to make informed decisions.

As a student affairs professional, having a strong understanding of AER will serve you well, since national trends point to greater accountability measures in higher education and, more specifically, student affairs. Thus, increased use of assessment, evaluation, and research to justify programming, uses of funding, and requests for future funding based on the impact to student learning and development will be essential. Moreover, both parents and students alike are questioning the worth of a college degree given the enormous costs, and national and regional accrediting bodies are requiring additional evidence of the educational impact on student learning. So, having working knowledge of the importance of AER is important to any higher education professional's success. Even before the current trends in higher education took hold, there was a strong push for increased assessment, evaluation, and research scholarship in student affairs.

Brief History: Call for Scholarship in Student Affairs

Hatfield and Wise (2015) in *A Guide to Becoming a Scholarly Practitioner in Student Affairs* documented this need for increased scholarship:

> Starting in 2001, both national student affairs organizations ACPA and NASPA and their respective journals have explored topics on scholarship in student affairs. There has been a call for more scholarship and expanding our view of scholarship. And in 2006, NASPA held a Summit on Scholarship (Jablonski, Mena, Manning, Carpenter, & Siko, 2006) that has served as a catalyst for reframing scholarship in student affairs. In addition, both NASPA and ACPA jointly approved Professional Competency Areas for Student Affairs Practitioners (2010) that includes using theories to inform our practice and contributing to the field through our reflections. (pp. 4–5)

As a result of this heightened attention and the concerted efforts by both NASPA and ACPA, the literature on student affairs scholarship has grown at an unprecedented rate, with 10 new books and a new journal between 2010 and 2016 (Henning, 2016).

The increased need for scholarship and the definitions for what constitutes scholarship are clearly defined in the work of Boyer (1990). In *Scholarship Reconsidered: Priorities of the Professoriate,* Boyer proposed an expansion in the definition of what constitutes scholarship into four separate but overlapping functions: the scholarship of discovery, the scholarship of integration, the scholarship of application, and the scholarship of teaching. The scholarship of discovery mirrors traditional definitions of scholarly research in which theory is tested and new knowledge generated. The scholarship of integration is the review of knowledge with the intent to generate new meanings, particularly across disciplines. The scholarship of application takes new knowledge from the process of discovery and the meanings derived from the process of integration to arrive at useful applications to extend the work. The scholarship of teaching takes into account the three previous levels of scholarship in translation to develop, deliver, and review teaching that most effectively helps students learn.

And while these four functions historically have represented an expansion of traditional faculty roles of teaching, service, and scholarship, this expansion is well documented as applicable to student affairs scholarship (Fried, 2002; Henning, 2016; Jablonski, 2005; Schroeder & Pike, 2001). Student affairs scholarship easily fits into Boyer's four-fold framework and into the intricate dance in which student affairs professionals engage using research to inform practice and practice to inform research. In *Student Affairs Scholarship (re?)considered: Toward a Scholarship of Practice,* Carpenter (2001) posited:

> Student affairs work consists of all kinds of scholarship borrowing from dozens of fields and facilitating environments in which education can make sense; wherein students can maximize their own learning, come to understand more about their place in the communities they interact with, and trust their own decision making at an even higher level, all the while creating patterns of personal development that will establish a foundation of lifelong learning. (p. 303)

Given this, student affairs professionals need to enter the field prepared to engage in assessment, evaluation, and research practices. By doing so, professionals will be able to anchor program design and delivery to theoretical foundations, to test the efficacy of chosen approaches in program design and delivery, to assess impacts on student learning and development, and to learn what works and does not work and modify programs and delivery accordingly.

Carpenter (2001) extended Boyer's framework to a set of 11 core values that constitutes good scholarship and that are equally applicable to assessment, evaluation, and research scholarship. Scholarship is intentional, theory-based, data-based, peer reviewed, tolerant of differing perspectives, collaborative, unselfish, open to change, careful and skeptical, attentive to regeneration, and autonomous within institutional contexts.

You should now have a better understanding of the differences in the types of scholarship and the intersections between Boyer's framework and quality scholarship in student affairs. Next, we will emphasize the professional benefits of engaging in scholarship.

The Benefits of AER Scholarship

Let us review why student affairs professionals would engage in scholarship. The very structure of engaging in scholarship requires you to be intentional about what questions need to be answered in the delivery of programs and services, to indicate how theory informs your program design, so that the data collected about program impacts are anchored in a foundation beyond just intuition as a practitioner. When you subject your scholarship to scrutiny through peer observation and more formalized peer review, it provides more objective insights into how to improve practice. The benefits are then numerous: improved programming and teaching practices, which in turn can improve student learning; increased answers as to what works and does not work and for whom, thus closing the assessment loop; and expansion of one's own professional identity development though increased skills, professional networks, and professional advancement opportunities. As you read earlier in this chapter, the push for accountability in higher education is not going away. The implications are too great not to engage as a means to communicate the differences that programs make in student learning and development. Stakeholders want to know our impact, and accreditors now require we report on our impact.

Develop a Scholarly Agenda

Let us turn our attention to the ways in which you can contribute to the research, scholarship, and expansion of knowledge within the profession. Developing a scholarly AER agenda may seem overwhelming at first blush, so begin by reviewing the work of other student affairs assessment scholars who have nicely paved the way for future scholarship. It is through reading the literature of these scholars and reflecting on the relevance to you as a professional that your own research agenda can unfold. As you will discover, the growth of scholarship of assessment began in earnest with the early works of Upcraft and

Schuh (1996) and Schuh and Upcraft (2000) and therein emerged the expanded role of the student affairs assessment professional. This growth in student affairs assessment continued though the 2000s with organizations like ACPA, NASPA, and Student Affairs Assessment Leaders (SAAL) leading the charge by defining standards for practice, creating communities of practice, and engaging professionals in discussions around practice and implementation. As you review the work of others, you are provided with rich examples of quality AER scholarship, and examples to help you in your own scholarly development. As the growth in assessment practice continues, so does the need for scholarship anchored to theoretical foundations, thus providing the foundation for quality practice.

Role of Theory

As noted earlier in this chapter, theory moves us from using just our intuition about what works and doesn't work to more formalized ways of establishing environments that help students learn and develop. What quality assessment, evaluation, and research share are well-thought-out (and critically examined) design grounded in a theoretical framework. Similarly, good scholarship is intentional, theory-based, and peer reviewed (Carpenter, 2001). While both informal and formal theories operate in the design, delivery, and assessment of student affairs' programs and services, an ongoing debate about the role of theory in student affairs practice continues (Reason & Kimball, 2012). Informal theories stem from "values, beliefs, and assumptions" (p. 360), whereas formal theories adhere to scholarly rigor because they are tested, scrutinized through peer review, and are generalizable due to replications. Examples of the latter are two educational theories frequently used to develop student affairs programming related to how students engage, learn, and develop: Alexander Astin's Theory of Student Involvement (1984) and Vincent Tinto's Theory of Student Departure (1993).

The Theory of Student Involvement posits that student engagement both academically and socially is essential for student success. Program staff must address the inputs, environment, and outcomes that affect student engagement to effectively use this theory. Inputs are what students bring to the learning environment, and include demographics and personal background that have shaped the student.

Environment includes each of the experiences students encounter in college, including involvement in and out of the classroom, and relationships. Outcomes are knowledge, attitudes, and beliefs that exist as shaped by the college experience.

The Theory of Student Departure explains why students leave higher education and informs programs and services on what they can do to retain students. Tinto (1993) posits that the three main reasons students leave are academic difficulties, inability to resolve their educational and occupational goals, and failure to become or remain incorporated in the intellectual and social life of the institution. To retain students, programs need to foster students' integration successfully into their academic studies, encourage their relationships with faculty and staff, engage them in extracurricular activities, and promote interactions with and foster belonging to peer groups.

As a professional, your goal is to bridge the gap between formal and informal theories by intertwining them in practice. As noted in Reason and Kimball (2012), "(A)ny successful model of theory to practice must attend to issues of rigor and adaptability as well as provide a mechanism to make explicit the hidden values, beliefs, and assumptions that undergird our practice, bringing these attributes into contact with formal theory through reflective practice" (p. 361). The assumptions held do shape practice, but it is formal theory that will allow one to test the degree to which assumptions hold and for whom, and to test assumptions by looking for both disconfirming and confirming evidence.

Research Ideas

There are multitudes of topics applicable to student affairs practice and scholarship to draw upon. *A Research and Scholarship Agenda for the Student Affairs Profession* (NASPA Task Force, 2011) offers "contemporary research topics, state-of-the-profession research topics, and professional competency research topics" (p. 2) into which student affairs professional can delve. This Agenda offers 12 contemporary topics ripe for research (pp. 5–12) and five state-of-the profession research topics (pp. 13–17), all listed with research questions to explore.

Contemporary research areas include

- Returning student veterans.

- Student mental health.
- Student development and evolving populations.
- Cost of higher education.
- Student affairs and community colleges.
- Emerging technologies.
- Implications for student affairs of institutional sustainability and viability.
- Globalization and internationalization.
- Social justice.
- History of student affairs.
- Student success and persistence.
- Student affairs leadership, administration, and organizational management.

State-of-the profession research areas include

- Student affairs perspectives on student affairs professionals (competencies, culture, skills, and knowledge).
- Quality of work life in student affairs.
- Characteristics and structures of student affairs divisions.
- Student affairs perspectives on students.
- Career goals and career paths of student affairs practitioners.

There are many other potential research topics to explore, especially those related to current issues that students face in higher education: higher education costs and diminished funding; access to higher education given costs; student engagement with changes in student demographics; student learning; student employment and career preparedness; and use of social networks, technology use, and online learning (Hamrick & Klein, 2015).

Professional Organizations

Conducting research can seem overwhelming, especially to the new professional, but you can expand AER knowledge though engagement in professional organizations and professional communities of practice. Opportunities abound in student affairs. The Council for the Advancement of Standards (CAS, 2015) in student affairs includes 42 member organizations that represent 45 functional areas across student affairs and many of these organizations hold national and regional conferences. Actively engaging in these organizations and their corresponding conferences offers many opportunities for collaborative scholarship. Moreover, NASPA and ACPA (as well as other student affairs organizations) offer active scholarship through publication outlets:

- NASPA has six journals that feature peer-reviewed research in student affairs (https://www.naspa.org/publications/journals).
- ACPA publishes "materials that are of timely assistance to student affairs practitioners in specific functional areas or topics of concern. ACPA Internal Publications reviews publication proposals for thought papers, guidance for good practice, handbooks for functional areas, and other guidebooks of demonstrated interest to student affairs practitioners" (http://www.myacpa.org/publications).

Finding an outlet for your scholarship is not difficult; the challenge may be getting to the place of creating scholarly work. Perhaps the easiest (and maybe most enjoyable) way to start is through viewing scholarship as a collaborative endeavor.

Scholarship as Collaboration

Student affairs professionals often collaborate with each other to build successful programming. Success in scholarship is no different. Graduate programs and divisions of student affairs can create strong partnerships that benefit both parties. Faculty in higher education programs can partner with student affairs colleagues, from the vice president to directors to program coordinators to graduate assistants, in conducting research and writing for publication. Graduate students and new professionals not well versed in the research process will learn skills ranging from writing a research protocol, submitting to the institutional review board, and conducting research ethically. Faculty will get the chance to work with graduate students who may be the closest to their research questions.

Another example is for graduate students in higher education to work with student affairs professional staff. Again, professionals know their work best, and so graduate students will be able to apply theoretical frameworks to lived situations to determine efficacy. This can be part of a sustained effort in the degree program to actually have students write and eventually determine an area of research.

As new professionals begin practice in higher education, the opportunity to engage with faculty aligns with the recent push towards more cocurricular programming and student success initiatives. The intersection of student and academic affairs in engaging and educating students offers a natural place from which to collaborate on scholarship.

There are a variety of outlets through which one can share work. We note some of these in the next section. The key is that if student affairs professionals seek to "do" assessment, research, and write, these activities will become part of the norm of the profession. When this happens, the profession and, more importantly students, will benefit from what we share.

Creating a Successful Partnership

As cocollaborators for several scholarly publications, we can attest to the fact that a successful scholarly partnership doesn't just happen: it is intentional. The most obvious point in forming a partnership is to pick a partner with whom you enjoy working, who shares your interests and curiosity about the same research topic, and is someone with whom you can have open and honest communication. Find a partner who has the subject matter expertise and/or skills that complement and expands your skill set too. For example, if you feel less equipped in research methods then find a partner to help you expand these skills.

Negotiate early in your relationship on your personal working and writing styles, and reach a place of agreement on writing formats (outlines, drafts, voice) and timelines for making progress on drafts and finished product. Discuss how you will solicit objective and constructive feedback on drafts and the final version before the formal submission process. Where will you keep all documents, versions, notes, and so on? Find a common electronic space and determine how you will know which version to work on.

Typically, one determines author order on the finished work at the onset of a writing project based on expected contributions and who initiated the research project. This can (and should) be renegotiated if the conditions change from those in the initial agreement. Remember, if you plan to publish or present research, you must seek institutional review board (IRB) approval first from the institution conducting the research. IRB protects the rights and welfare of human research subjects recruited to participate in research activities. If you and your partner(s) are from different institutions, you may need IRB approval from each of them; talk to your IRB and find out. There may be an exemption status for your work depending on what you are planning to do; however, only IRB can determine this, so you must submit a protocol for your proposed work before you begin.

Presenting and Publishing Outlets

Student affairs professionals often love attending conferences. The discipline offers plenty of opportunities to network with colleagues and learn what other institutions are doing and prioritizing. We recommend submitting a proposal to present at one of them. If you have never presented before, you can choose to aim big and propose a session for an annual NASPA or ACPA conference. Even if your proposal is not accepted, you will have gained the experience of submitting. Frankly, there are plenty of regional and even local meetings that offer smaller crowds, but just as important work.

If standing in front of a group of people frightens you, you can opt to present with a colleague. Conferences also offer panels, roundtables, and poster sessions. Find a conference that fits you and then explore the options for the kinds of sharing that work for you.

In addition to presenting at conferences, academics are constantly researching and writing. Their curricula vitae (CVs) enumerate the many journals in which they have published, including those that have been peer-reviewed (the gold standard) and those that were less rigorously reviewed, if reviewed at all. The peer-review process, which funnels one's work through an editorial review of experts in the field and an editorial board, can be lengthy and intimidating. Thus, it may behoove you to begin with submitting to publications with less strenuous processes.

Hatfield and Wise (2015) refer to a schema developed by Professor Danelle Stevens of the Graduate School of Education at Portland State University. Stevens calls a third-generation journal one that is not necessarily peer-reviewed and often practitioner-friendly. In other words, these journals share better practices of what people are doing in their work. Examples of a third-generation journal include ACPA's *About Campus* and NASPA's *Leadership Exchange*. In addition, specific areas of student affairs such as student unions, advising, and recreation centers have third-generation publications that welcome insights. This is in contrast to first-generation journals that are peer reviewed, entail original research, require use of accepted practices of methodology, are formatted in a typical academic manner, and whose main audience are researchers. *The Journal of Student Affairs Research and Practice* as well as the *Journal of College Student Development* fall into this category. We often think of these kinds of journals when we first venture into publishing. Lastly, second-generation journals are those that are somewhere in between the other two, often including articles that summarize others' research.

One place to start within a journal is to pen a book review. Often, journals will publish different kinds of manuscripts that run the gamut from original research to writing about newly published books relevant to the field. Writing a book review is a much less threatening foray into the publication process. Find journals in your area, read a few to determine what kinds of writing they accept, and if they have a book review section, contact the editor and determine if you can propose a book or if the publication has some in mind. Regardless of what kind of article you wish to write, make sure you carefully read the publication guidelines and follow them exactly.

In addition to journals, numerous other outlets are available where your voice can be heard and your practice shared. Blogs and online newsletters are ubiquitous now, so if you find one that matches your passion, then contact the owner of the page or organization. If you see a gap and are not finding an outlet for what you really want to say, you can easily begin your own site through various resources such as WordPress, Weebly, or Canva.

Embarking on a New Career

As you search for a meaningful institutional partner with whom to share your passion for student affairs work, consider asking prospective employers their thoughts on the role of scholarship. Are there expectations in place for student affairs professionals to present at conferences or write blog posts or journal articles? If not, inquire about being given the autonomy to do so, particularly if you are expected to collaborate with others in student and academic affairs. You could even add this to the list of common interview questions you should ask regarding professional development opportunities.

If you already have a portfolio of oral and written work to show your prospective employer, then good for you. If you do not, consider beginning one. It is important to note these on your resume, but also be prepared to show off your effective communication skills through concrete examples, particularly if you have partnered with others in the process.

Examples of Scholarship Engagement in Practice

Opportunities abound in student affairs to engage in scholarship through assessment practice. As indicated earlier, CAS Standards (2015) represent 45 functional areas across student affairs and many of these organizations hold national and regional conferences. You can be assured of working in one of these areas, if employed in student affairs. Assessment occurs within departments and it also occurs at the division level for larger initiatives, ones that would involve collaboration across functional areas. Presented are two examples of how professionals in differing student affairs areas moved from theory to practice to scholarship.

Functional area example. Advising Services within the Division of Student Affairs at Hatfield-Wise University has chosen to use the CAS Self-Assessment Guide for Academic Advising Programs in its program redesign process. The Director determined that all Advising Services programming and assessment planning moving forward would be anchored in a theoretical foundation and adhere to standards of best practice. CAS and related guidelines for Academic Advising Programs (AAP) represent both of these, as their general foundations derive from numerous member organizations and also represent National Academic Advising Association (NACADA) core values for practice (2005). CAS provides the framework for those in student affairs to develop "programs, services and experiences that contribute to student learning experiences that are valued at their institution and, moreover, that are empirically verified as adding value to the student experience at their institutions" (Schuh & Gansemer-Topf, 2010, p. 6).

The Director formed an assessment team including staff members, a graduate intern, and an Associate Director. The team developed an assessment plan that included learning and development outcomes, one from each of the six CAS learning domains, and then specified a plan to assess each outcome. The student learning and development domains included knowledge acquisition, construction, integration and application; cognitive complexity; intrapersonal development; interpersonal competence; humanitarianism and civic engagement; and practical competence.

The Director of Advising along with team members have written about their process, and included the foundations in both theory and practice that shaped the creation of their new program plan. The Director submitted the paper to a student affairs third-generation, practitioner-based journal.

Divisional initiative example. Also at Hatfield-Wise University, its Division of Student Affairs decided to work on a division-wide initiative *Building Foundations for the Healthy Campus*. The Division's assessment coordinator formed a research team consisting of staff members and associate directors. The Division team began its process by researching national policy and standards for practice under the national Healthy Campus 2020/ Healthy People 2020 plans. They then engaged in a number of activities and discussions to develop a five-phase process to tackle the initiative:

Phase 1: Articulate initiative vision, mission, and goals.
Phase 2: Collect baseline data.
Phase 3: Develop objectives.
Phase 4: Develop an action plan and track progress.
Phase 5: Synthesize, interpret and present findings.

They determined that by going through this process, they could then apply this same framework to any future initiatives. They decided to participate in a national consortium study to collect benchmark data to track their progress over time and to form comparisons with peer institutions. The baseline assessment, ACHA-National College Health Assessment (NCHA), a nationally recognized research survey, also aligned to relevant research underlying Healthy Campus 2020 and Healthy People 2020. They submitted an IRB proposal because they knew the results would be used for external use.

They developed an action plan after the data were analyzed and interpreted and benchmarks established. In addition, the team developed a conference proposal presenting their findings and later wrote an article published in the *Journal of Student Affairs Research and Practice.* Because of their quality practices, their research passed the scrutiny of peer review.

Self-Reflection Exercise: Steps to Develop a Proposal or Paper

Try engaging in this process to kick-start your scholarship practices.

Step 1: Read through journals and conference proposals.	*What venue do you wish to write toward?*
	Read publishing and presenting guidelines.
	Make sure you understand what you will need to submit.
	Contact editors or reviewers if you're not sure.
Step 2: Identify your professional areas of passion.	*What lights up your mind?*
	Choose two or three topics within those areas.
	Set the timer for 10 minutes and free write about these topics.
	A directed free write is when you keep writing whatever pops in your head about the topic at hand, so put pen to paper or fingers to keyboard and keep writing until time is up.
	Don't worry about grammatical conventions, spelling, or lofty vocabulary. Write about whatever comes to mind.
	What do these topics make you think of? Do you see any connections to other topics? What questions do you have?
Step 3: Select one topic to explore in more depth.	*What topic deserves furthering exploring?*
	Read through relevant research.
	Take notes on questions that emerge from your readings.
	Identify questions that would be of interest to the larger professional community.

Step 4: Select a mentor or your supervisor to advance your writing.	***Who do you trust to give you constructive feedback and positive support?***
	Determine if you will have a collaborator.
	Identify the presentation/publishing outlets that feel most comfortable for you.
	Review the guidelines for presenting/publishing.
Step 5: Write an outline for your topic.	***What is your style of outlining?***
	Understand the audience served by your selected presentation/publication outlet.
	Address required sections for your presentation/publication.
Step 6: Develop a schedule for writing.	***Don't wait for inspiration!***
	Commit to this schedule with your co-writer, mentor, or your supervisor.
	Work in time for feedback and revisions.
Step 7: Find your voice.	***How will your voice come through your work?***
	Does it have to be an academic voice?
	What makes this presentation/publication uniquely you and not someone you have read or researched?
Step 8: Double check.	***Have you met all the requirements for your selected presentation/publication outlet?***

REFERENCES

ACT (n.d.). Retrieved from http://www.act.org/content/dam/act/unsecured/documents/WK-Brief-KeyFacts-CognitiveandNoncognitiveSkills.pdf

Adams-Gaston, J., & Kennedy-Phillips, L. C. (2015). Tenet six: Anchor cultural change. In R. P. Bingham, D. A. Bureau, & A. G. Duncan (Eds.), *Leading assessment for student success: Ten tenets that change culture and practice in student affairs,* 70–78. Sterling, VA: Stylus Publishing.

Adelman, C., Ewell, P., Gaston, P., & Schneider, C. G. (2011). *The degree qualifications profile.* Indianapolis, IN: Lumina Foundation.

Alexander, L. (1986). Time for results: An overview. *The Phi Delta Kappan, 68,* 202–204.

Alexander, L., Clinton, B., & Kean, T. H. (1986). *Time for results: The governors' 1991 report on education.* Washington, DC: National Governors' Association.

Altbach, P. G. (1991). Patterns in higher education development: Toward the year 2000. *The Review of Higher Education, 14,* 293–315.

American Association for Higher Education. (1992). *Nine principles of good practice for assessing student learning.* North Kansas City, MO: AAHE.

American Association for Higher Education, American College Personnel Association, & National Association of Student Personnel Administrators. (1998). *Powerful partnerships: A shared responsibility for learning. A joint report.* Washington, DC: Authors.

American Association for Higher Education. (2000). *Principles of good practice for assessing student learning.* Washington, DC: Author.

American College Personnel Association. (1994). *The student learning imperative: Implications for student affairs.* Washington, DC: Author.

American College Personnel Association. (2006). *ASK standards: Assessment skills and knowledge content standards for student affairs practitioners and scholars.* Washington, DC: Author.

American College Personnel Association & National Association of Student Personnel Administrators. (1997). *The principles of good practice for student affairs.* Washington, DC: Authors.

American College Personnel Association & National Association of Student Personnel Administrators. (2010). *ACPA/NASPA professional competency areas for student affairs practitioners.* Washington, DC: Authors.

American College Personnel Association & National Association of Student Personnel Administrators. (2011). *ACPA/NASPA professional competency rubrics.* Washington, DC: Authors.

American College Personnel Association & National Association of Student Personnel Administrators. (2015). *ACPA/NASPA professional competency areas for student affairs educators.* Washington, DC: Authors.

American College Personnel Association & National Association of Student Personnel Administrators. (2016). *ACPA/NASPA professional competency rubrics.* Washington, DC: Authors.

American Council on Education. (1937). *Student personnel point of view.* Washington, DC: Author.

American Council on Education. (1949). *Student personnel point of view* (2nd ed.). Washington, DC: Author.

American Educational Research Association, American Psychological Association, & National Council on Measurement in Education, & Joint Committee on Standards for Educational and Psychological Testing. (2014). *Standards for educational and psychological testing.* Washington, DC: AERA.

American Educational Research Association. (2011). Code of ethics. Washington, DC: Author. Retrieved from http://www.aera.net/Portals/38/docs/About_AERA/CodeOfEthics(1).pdf

Anderson, L. W., & Krathwohl, D. R. (2001). *A taxonomy for learning, teaching, and assessing: A revision of Bloom's taxonomy of educational objectives.* New York: Longman.

Armstrong, D., Gosling, A., Weinman, J., & Marteau, T. (1997). The place of inter-rater reliability in qualitative research: an empirical study. *Sociology, 31,* 597–606.

Ashcroft, J. (1986). Does a degree tell us what a student has learned? *The Phi Delta Kappan, 68,* 225–227.

Association for American Colleges. (1985). *Integrity in the college curriculum: A report to the academic community.* Washington, DC: Author.

Association of American Colleges and Universities. (2011). *The LEAP vision for learning: Outcomes, practices, impact, and employers' views.* Washington, DC: AAC&U. Retrieved from https://www.aacu.org/sites/default/files/files/LEAP/leap_vision_summary.pdf

Association of American Colleges & Universities (AAC&U), & National Leadership Council (NLC) (US). (2007). *College learning for the new global century: A report from the National Leadership Council for Liberal Education &*

America's Promise. Washington, DC: Association of American Colleges & Universities.

Association for Institutional Research. (2013, May 2). *Code of ethics and professional practice (CODE).* Retrieved from Association for Institutional Research (AIR) website: https://www.airweb.org/Membership/Pages /CodeOfEthics.aspx

Astin, A. W. (1984). Student involvement: A developmental theory for higher education. *Journal of College Student Development, 25,* 297–308.

Azusa Pacific University. (n.d.). Revised Bloom's taxonomy verb list. Retrieved from https://www.apu.edu/live_data/files/333/blooms_taxonomy _action_verbs.pdf

Babbie, E., & Mouton, J. (2001). *The practice of social research.* Cape Town: Oxford University Press.

Banta, T. W. (Ed.). (2002). *Building a scholarship of assessment.* San Francisco: Jossey-Bass.

Banta, T. W., & Blaich, C. (2011). Closing the assessment loop. *Change: The Magazine of Higher Learning, 43*(1), 22–27.

Banta, T. W., & Palomba, C. A. (2015). *Assessment essentials: Planning, implementing, and improving assessment in higher education* (2nd ed.). San Francisco: Jossey-Bass.

Barber, J. P. (2006). Tenet two: Commit to student learning as a primary focus. In R. P. Bingham, D. Bureau, & A. G. Duncan (Eds.), *Leading assessment for student success* (pp. 22–39). Sterling, VA: Stylus.

Barr, R. B., & Tagg. J. (1995). From teaching to learning—a new paradigm for undergraduate education. *Change: The Magazine of Higher Learning, 12–* 25.

Baxter Magolda, M. B. (1992). *Knowing and reasoning in college: Gender-related patterns in students' intellectual development.* San Francisco: Jossey-Bass.

Baxter Magolda, M. B., & Magolda, P. M. (2011). What counts as "essential" knowledge for student affairs educators? In P. M. Magolda & M. B. Baxter Magolda (Eds.), *Contested issues in student affairs: Diverse perspectives and respectful dialogue* (pp. 3–14). Sterling, VA: Stylus.

Benson, J. (1996). Developing a strong program of construct validation: A test anxiety example. *Educational Measurement: Issues and Practice, 17,* 10– 17.

Bettencourt, G. M., Malaney, V. K., Kidder, C. J., & George Mwangi, C. A. (2017). Examining scholar-practitioner identity in peer-led research communities in higher education programs. *Journal for the Study of Postsecondary and Tertiary Education, 2,* 95–113. https://doi.org/10.28945 /3783

Bingham, R. P., Bureau, D. A., & Duncan, A. G. (2015). *Leading assessment for student success: Ten tenets that change culture and practice in student affairs.* Sterling, VA: Stylus.

Blaich, C., & Wise, K. (2011). *From gathering to using assessment results: Lessons from the Wabash National Study.* NILOA Occasional Paper No. 8). Urbana, IL: University of Illinois and Indiana University, National Institute for Learning Outcomes Assessment.

Blimling, G. S., & Whitt, E. J. (1999). *Good practice in student affairs: Principles to foster student learning.* San Francisco: Jossey-Bass.

Bloland, P. A. (1991, March). *A brief history of student development.* Paper presented at the Annual Convention of the American College Personnel Association, Atlanta, GA. Retrieved from http://files.eric.ed.gov/fulltext/ED350520.pdf

Bloom, B. S. (1956). *Taxonomy of educational objectives: The classification of educational goals.* London: Longmans, Green.

Bowman, N. A. (2013). Understanding and addressing the challenges of assessing college student growth in student affairs. *Research & Practice in Assessment, 8*(2), 5–14.

Boyer, E. L. (1990). *Scholarship reconsidered: Priorities of the professoriate.* Princeton, NJ: The Carnegie Foundation for the Advancement of Teaching.

Bresciani, M. J. (December, 2003). *Identifying projects that deliver outcomes and provide a means of assessment: A concept mapping checklist.* National Association for Student Personnel Administrators, Inc., NetResults E-Zine. Retrieved from https://www.pdx.edu/institutional-assessment-council/sites/www.pdx.edu.institutional-assessment-council/files/Concept%20Mapping%20Bresciani.pdf

Bresciani, M. J. (2010). Understanding barriers to student affairs professionals' engagement in outcomes-based assessment of student learning and development. *Journal of Student Affairs, 14,* 81–90.

Bresciani, M. J., Moore Gardner, M., & Hickmott, J. (2009). *Demonstrating student success: A practical guide to outcomes-based assessment of learning and development in student affairs.* Sterling, VA: Stylus.

Bresciani, M., Zelna, C., & Anderson, J.A. (2004). *Assessing student learning and development: A handbook for practitioners.* Washington, DC: National Association of Student Personnel Administrators (NASPA).

Brown, R. D. (1972). Student development in tomorrow's higher education: A return to the academy. *Student Personnel Series, 16,* 1–55. Retrieved from www.myacpa.org.

Carpenter, S. (2001). Student affairs scholarship (re?)considered: Toward a scholarship of practice. *Journal of College Student Development, 42*(4), 301–318.

Centers for Disease Control and Prevention. (2013). *Evaluating reporting: A guide to help ensure use of evaluation findings*. Atlanta, GA: U.S. Department of Health and Human Services.

Check, J., & Schutt, R. K. (2011). *Research methods in education*. Thousand Oaks, CA: Sage.

Cicchetti, D. V. (1994). Guidelines, criteria, and rules of thumb for evaluating normed and standardized assessment instruments in psychology. *Psychological Assessment, 6,* 284–290.

Clark, J., & Brown, S. (2017). Connecting assessment and strategic planning to advancing equity on campus. *The Journal of Student Affairs Inquiry, 2*(1).

Cohen, J. (1992). A power primer. *Psychological Bulletin, 112*(1), 155–159.

Cohen, L., Manion, L., & Morrison, K. (2013). *Research methods in education*. New York: Routledge.

Council for the Advancement of Standards in Higher Education. (2009). CAS learning and development outcomes. Retrieved from http://www.cas.edu/learningoutcomes

Council for the Advancement of Standards in Higher Education. (2015). *CAS professional standards for higher education* (9th ed.). Washington, DC: Author.

Council for the Advancement of Standards in Higher Education. (2017). *Assessment Services Standards and Guidelines*. Available from http://www.cas.edu/store_product.asp?prodid=113

Creswell, J. W., & Miller, D. L. (2000). Determining validity in qualitative inquiry. *Theory into Practice, 39*(3), 124–130.

Creswell, J. W. (2014). *Research design: qualitative, quantitative, and mixed methods approaches*. Los Angeles: Sage.

Culp, M. M. (2012). Establishing a culture of evidence foundation. In M. M. Culp & G. J. Dungy (Eds.), *Building a culture of evidence in student affairs: A guide for leaders and practitioners* (pp. 21–34). Washington, DC: NASPA.

Duncan, (2015, June). Beware spurious correlations. *Harvard Business Review.* Retrieved from https://hbr.org/2015/06/beware-spurious-correlations.

Education Commission of the States. (1986). *Transforming the state role in undergraduate education: Time for a different view*. Denver, CO: Author.

Erwin, T. D., & Wise, S. L. (2002). A scholar-practitioner model for assessment. In T. W. Banta & Associates (Eds.), *Building a scholarship of assessment* (pp. 67–81). San Francisco: Jossey-Bass.

Evans, N. J., Forney, D. S., Guido, F. M., Patton, L. D., & Renn, K. A. (2010). *Student development in college: Theory, research, and practice* (2nd ed.). San Francisco: Jossey-Bass.

Ewell, P. T. (1991). To capture the ineffable: New forms of assessment in higher education. *Review of Research in Education, 17,* 75–125.

Ewell, P. T. (2002). An emerging scholarship: A brief history of assessment. In T. W. Banta & Associates (Eds.), *Building a scholarship of assessment* (pp. 3–25). San Francisco: Jossey-Bass.

Ewell, P. T. (2009). *Assessment, accountability, and improvement: Revisiting the tension* (NILOA Occasional Paper No.1). Urbana, IL: University of Illinois and Indiana University, National Institute for Learning Outcomes Assessment.

Fernandez, D., Fitzgerald, C., Hambler, V., & Mason-Innes, T. (2016). *CACUSS student affairs and services competency model.* Retrieved from https://www.cacuss.ca/files/Competency-Docs/CACUSS_Student _Affairs_and_Services_Competency_Model_FINAL.pdf

Fried, J. (2002). The scholarship of student affairs: Integration and application. *NASPA Journal, 39,* 120–31.

Fulcher, K. H., Good, M. R., Coleman, C. M., & Smith, K. L. (2014). *A simple model for learning improvement: Weigh pig, feed pig, weigh pig.* (NILOA Occasional Paper No. 23). Urbana, IL: University of Illinois and Indiana University, National Institute for Learning Outcomes Assessment.

Fulcher, K. H., Smith, K. L., Sanchez, E., Ames, A. J., & Meixner, C. (2017). Return of the pig: Standards for learning improvement. *Research & Practice in Assessment, 11,* 10–40.

Gansemer-Topf, A. M., & Kennedy-Phillips, L. C. (2017). Assessment and evaluation. In J. H. Schuh, S. R. Jones, & V. Torres (Eds.), *Student services: A handbook for the profession* (6th ed.), 327–343.

Gardner, D. P. (1983). *A nation at risk.* [Archived Information]. Retrieved from: https://www2.ed.gov/pubs/NatAtRisk/risk.html

Godlewska, A., Massey, J., Adjei, J., & Moore, J. (2013). The unsustainable nature of ignorance: Measuring knowledge to effect social change. First results of an on-line survey of Aboriginal knowledge in an Ontario university. *The Canadian Journal of Native Studies, 33*(1), 65–95. Retrieved from https://search.proquest.com/openview/e77cf8a61d9e44bb15f79719 d45302d4/1

Godlewska, A., Schaefli, L., Massey, J., Freake, S., Adjei, J. K., Rose, J., & Hudson, C. (2017). What do first-year university students in Newfoundland and Labrador know about Aboriginal peoples and topics? *The Canadian Geographer, 61,* 579–594. doi: 10.1111/cag.12428.

Golafshani, N. (2003). Understanding reliability and validity in qualitative research. *The Qualitative Report, 8*(4), 597–606.

Great Schools Partnership (2013). The Glossary of Education Reform. Retrieved from https://www.edglossary.org/co-curricular/

Guldbrandsson, K., & Fossum, B. (2009). An exploration of the theoretical concepts, policy windows, and policy entrepreneurs at the Swedish public health arena. *Health Promotion International, 24*(4), 434–444.

Haave, N. (2014, June 14). *Six questions that will bring your teaching philosophy into focus.* Retrieved from https://www.facultyfocus.com/articles/philosophy-of-teaching/six-questions-will-bring-teaching-philosophy-focus/

Hammersley, M. (1992). *What's wrong with ethnography?* London: Routledge.

Hamrick, F. A., & Klein, K. (2015). Trends and milestones affecting student affairs practice. *New Directions for Student Services, 151,* 15–25.

Hamrick, F. A., Evans, N. J., & Schuh, J. H. (2002). *Foundations of student affairs practice: How philosophy, theory, and research strengthen educational outcomes.* San Francisco: John Wiley & Sons.

Hatfield, L. J., & Wise, V. L. (2015). *A guide to becoming a scholarly practitioner in student affairs.* Sterling, VA: Stylus.

Henning, G. W. (2016). *The scholarship of student affairs assessment reconsidered.* Retrieved from https://jsai.scholasticahq.com/article/780-the-scholarship-of-student-affairs-assessment-reconsidered

Henning, G. W., Mitchell, A. A., & Maki, P. L. (2008). The assessment skills and knowledge standards. Professionalizing the work of assessing student learning and development. *About Campus, 13*(4), 11–17.

Henning, G. W., & Roberts, D. (2016). *Student affairs assessment: Theory to practice.* Sterling, VA: Stylus.

Herdlein, R., Kline, K., Boquard, B., & Haddad, V. (2010). A survey of faculty perceptions of learning outcomes in master's level programs in higher education and student affairs. *College Student Affairs Journal, 29,* 33–45.

Herdlein, R., Riefler, L., & Mrowka, K. (2013). An integrative literature review of student affairs competencies: A meta-analysis. *Journal of Student Affairs Research and Practice, 50,* 250–269.

Hoffman, J. L., & Bresciani, M. J. (2010). Assessment work: Examining the prevalence and nature of learning assessment competencies and skills in student affairs job postings. *Journal of Student Affairs Research and Practice, 47,* 495–512.

Hoffman, J. L., & Bresciani, M. J. (2012). Identifying what student affairs professionals value: A mixed methods analysis of professional competencies listed in job descriptions. *Research & Practice in Assessment, 7,* 26–40.

Holland, J. L. (1997). *Making vocational choices: A theory of vocational personalities and work environments* (3rd ed.). Odessa, FL: Psychological Assessment Resources. http://www.learningoutcomeassessment.org/documents/Wabash_001.pdf

Hutchings, P., Ewell, P., & Banta, T. (2013). *AAHE principles of good practice: Aging nicely.* Champaign, IL: NILOA. Retrieved from http://www.learningoutcomeassessment.org/PrinciplesofAssessment.html#AAHE

Jablonski, M. A., Mena, S. B., Manning, K., Carpenter, S., & Siko, K. L. (2006). Scholarship in student affairs revisited: The summit on scholarship, March 2006. *NASPA Journal, 43*(4), 182–201.

Jablonski, M. A. (2005). Where is the scholarship in student affairs? *NASPA Journal, 42*(2), 147–152.

Kane, M. T. (2001). Current concerns in validity theory. *Journal of Educational Measurement, 38*(4), 319–342.

Kane, M. T. (2010). Validity and fairness. *Language testing, 27*(2), 177–182.

Kane, M. T. (2013). The argument-based approach to validation. *School Psychology Review, 42*(4), 448–457.

Keeling, R. P. (Ed.). (2004). *Learning reconsidered: A campus-wide focus on the student experience.* Washington, DC: National Association of Student Personnel Administrators and the American College Personnel Association.

Keeling, R. P. (2006). *Learning reconsidered 2: Implementing a campus-wide focus on the student experience.* Washington, DC: National Association of Student Personnel Administrators and the American College Personnel Association.

Keith, K. M. (2008). *The case for servant leadership.* Westfield, IN: Greenleaf Center for Servant Leadership.

Kennesaw State University. (n.d.). *Improve KSU: Assessment plan and improvement report template.* Retrieved from http://oie.kennesaw.edu/improve-ksu/docs/Improve%20KSU%20Template%20Revised.pdf.

Kezar, A. J. (2000). Higher education research at the millennium: Still trees without fruit? *The Review of Higher Education, 23*(4), 443–468. https://doi.org/10.1353
/rhe.2000.0018

Kingdon, J.W. (2001). *A model of agenda-setting with applications.* Washington, DC: Quello Telecommunications Policy and Law Symposium.

Kingdon, J.W. (2010). *Agendas, alternatives, and public policies* (3rd ed.). New York: Longman.

Kirkpatrick, D. L. (1979). Techniques for evaluating training programs. *Training and Development Journal, 33*(6), 78–92.

Kirkpatrick, D. L. (1994). *Evaluating training programs: The four levels* (2nd ed.). San Francisco: Berrett-Koehler.

Kolb, D. A. (1984). *Experiential learning: Experience as the source of learning and development.* Englewood Cliffs, NJ: Prentice-Hall.

Kotter, J. P., & Cohen, D. S. (2002). *The heart of change: Real-life stories of how people change their organizations.* Boston: Harvard Business Review Press.

Kouzes, J. M., & Posner, B. Z. (2017). *The leadership challenge* (6th ed.). Hoboken, NJ: John Wiley & Sons.

Kuh, G. D., Gonyea, R. M., & Rodriguez, D. P. (2002). The scholarly assessment of student development. In T. W. Banta & Associates (Eds.), *Building a scholarship of assessment* (pp. 100–127). San Francisco: Jossey-Bass.

Kuh, G. D., Ikenberry, S. O., Jankowski, N. A., Cain, T. R., Ewell, P. T, Hutchings, P., & Kinzie, J. (2015). *Using evidence of student learning to improve higher education.* San Francisco: Jossey-Bass.

Lave, J., & Wenger, E. (1991). *Situated learning: Legitimate peripheral participation.* New York: Cambridge University Press.

Lazarsfeld, P.F. (1959). Problems in methodology. In R. K. Merton, L. Bloom, and L. S. Cottrell, Jr. (Eds.) *Sociology today: Problems and perspectives* (39–78). New York: Basic Books.

LeCompte M. D., & Preissle, J. (1993). *Ethnography and qualitative design in educational research.* San Diego, CA: Academic Press.

Lincoln, Y. S., & Guba, E. G. (1985). *Naturalistic Inquiry.* Newbury Park, CA: Sage.

Little, J. A., & Rubin, D. B. (2002). *Statistical analysis with missing data* (2nd ed.). Hoboken, NJ: John Wiley& Sons.

Lodico, M. G., Spaudling, D. T., & Voegtle, K. H. (2006). *Methods in educational research: From theory to practice.* San Francisco: Jossey-Bass.

Maki, P. L. (2004). *Assessing for learning: Building a sustainable commitment across the institution.* Sterling, VA: Stylus.

Martin, J. (1992). *Cultures in organizations: Three perspectives.* New York: Oxford University Press.

Mason, J. (2002). Organizing and indexing qualitative data. In Mason, J. (Eds.), *Qualitative researching* (2nd ed, p. 147–172). London: Sage.

Massey, J., Sulak, T., & Sriram, R. (2013). Influences of theory and practice in the development of servant leadership in students. *Journal of Leadership Education, 12*(1), 74–91.

Massey, K. D. (2017). *Professional identity in Canadian student affairs and services.* (Unpublished doctoral dissertation). University of Texas at Austin, Austin, TX.

Messick, S. (1989). Validity. In R. L. Linn (Ed.), *Educational measurement* (pp. 13–103). New York: Macmillan.

Middaugh, M. F. (2010). *Planning and assessment in higher education: Demonstrating institutional effectiveness.* San Francisco: Jossey-Bass.

NACADA. (2005). *NACADA statement of core values of academic advising.* Retrieved from the NACADA Clearinghouse of Academic Advising Resources website: http://www.nacada.ksu.edu/Resources/Clearing house/View-Articles/Core-values-of-academic-advising.aspx

NASPA Task Force. (2011). *A research and scholarship agenda for the student affairs profession.* Retrieved from https://nasparegion5.files.wordpress .com/2012/02/naspa-research-agenda.pdf

National Institute of Education. (1984). *Involvement in learning: Realizing the potential of American higher education.* Washington, DC: U.S. Department of Education.

National Institute for Learning Outcomes Assessment. (2011). Transparency framework. Urbana, IL: University of Illinois and Indiana University, National Institute for Learning Outcomes Assessment (NILOA). Retrieved from http://www.learningoutcomesassessment.org/Transparency Framework.htm

Oaks, D. J. (2015). Mapping to curricular and institutional goals. *New Directions for Institutional Research, 164,* 51–60.

Ortiz, A. M., Filimon, I., & Cole-Jackson, M. (2015). Preparing student affairs educators. In J. H. Schuh, & E. J. Whitt (Eds.), *New directions for student services, 1997–2014* (pp. 81–90). San Francisco: Jossey-Bass.

Palomba, C. A., & Banta, T. W. (1999). *Assessment essentials: Planning, implementing, and improving assessment in higher education.* San Francisco: Jossey-Bass.

Paulhus, D. L., & Vazire, S. (2007). The self-report method. In R. C. Fraley & R. F. Krueger (Eds.), *Handbook of research methods in personality psychology* (pp. 224–239). New York: Guilford.

Pelletier, J., Oaks, D. J., & Kennedy-Phillips, L. C. (2013). Grounded in reality: Writing learning outcomes. *The Bulletin, 81*(6).

Popper, K. (1963). *Conjectures and refutations: The growth of scientific knowledge.* Reprinted 2004. New York: Routledge.

Reason. R. D., & Kimball, E. W. (2012). A new theory-to-practice model for student affairs: Integrating scholarship, context, and reflection. *Journal of Student Affairs Research and Practice, 49*(4), 359–376.

Reynolds, C. R., & Ramsay, M. C. (2003). Bias in psychological assessment: An empirical review and recommendations. In J. R. Graham & J. A. Naglieri (Eds.), *Handbook of psychology: Assessment psychology* (Vol. 10, pp. 67–93). Hoboken, NJ: Wiley.

Rhine, L., Martinez-Saenz, M., & Davenport, Z. R., (2012). The student success conundrum. In B. Bontrager (Ed.), *Strategic management of college enrollments.* Washington, DC: AACRAO.

Rhodes, T. (2009). *Assessing outcomes and improving achievement: Tips and tools for using the rubrics.* Washington, DC: Association of American Colleges and Universities.

Ritchie, J., Lewis, J., Nicholls, C. M., & Ormston, R. (Eds.). (2013). *Qualitative research practice: A guide for social science students and researchers.* London: Sage.

Robbins, S. B., Lauver, K., Le, H., Davis, D., Langley, R., & Carlstrom, A. (2004). Do psychosocial and study skill factors predict college outcomes.? A meta-analysis. *Psychological Bulletin, 130*(2), 261–288.

Rosenberg, M., & Simmons, R. G. (1971). *Black and white self-esteem: The urban school child.* Washington, DC: American Sociological Association.

Ross, L. E., & Lewis, J. R. (2017). *Data-informed decision cultures.* Course paper: A holistic approach to institutional research. Tallahassee, FL: Association for Institutional Research.

Ryder, A. J., & Kimball, E. W. (2015). Assessment as reflexive practice: A grounded model for making evidence-based decisions in student affairs. *Research & Practice in Assessment, 10,* 30–45.

Sandeen, A., & Barr, M.J. (2006). *Critical issues for student affairs.* San Francisco: Jossey-Bass.

Schein, E. H. (1992). *Organizational culture and leadership* (2nd ed.). San Francisco: Jossey-Bass.

Schroeder, C. C., & Pike, G. R. (2001). The scholarship of application in student affairs. *Journal of College Student Development, 42*(4), 342–355.

Schuh, J. H., & Gansemer-Topf, A. M. (2010). *The role of student affairs in student learning assessment.* Urbana, IL: University of Illinois and Indiana University, National Institute for Learning Outcomes Assessment.

Schuh, J. H., Biddix, J. P., Dean, L. A., & Kinzie, J. (2016). *Assessment in student affairs* (2nd ed.). San Francisco: John Wiley & Sons.

Schuh, J. H., & Upcraft, M. L. (1998). Facts and myths about assessment in student affairs. *About Campus, 3*(5), 2–8.

Schuh, J. H., & Upcraft, M. L. (2000). *Assessment practice in student affairs: An applications manual.* San Francisco: Jossey-Bass.

Schuh, J. H., Upcraft, M. L., & Associates (2001). *Assessment practice in student affairs: An application manual.* San Francisco: Jossey-Bass.

Schuh, J. H., & Associates (2009). *Assessment methods for student affairs.* San Francisco: Jossey-Bass.

Schuh, J. H., Biddix, J. P., Dean, L. A., & Kinzie, J. (2016). *Assessment in student affairs* (2nd ed.). San Francisco: Jossey-Bass.

Sharp, M. D. (2017). Overview of the CAS Professional Standards. In N. Y. Gulley, S. R. Dean, & L. A. Dean (Eds). *Using the CAS Professional Standards: Diverse examples of practice* (pp. 1–16). Washington, DC: NASPA, ACPA, CAS.

Shutt, M. D., Garrett, J. M., Lynch, J. W., & Dean, L. A. (2012). An assessment model as best practice in student affairs. *Journal of Student Affairs Research and Practice, 49*(1), 65–82.

Sinek, S. (2011). *Start with why: How great leaders inspire everyone to take action.* New York, NY: Penguin.

Sriram, R. (2011). Engaging research as a student affairs professional. *Net Results: Critical issues for student affairs practitioners.* Retrieved from https://works.bepress.com/rishi_sriram/10/download/

Sriram, R., & Oster, M. (2012). Reclaiming the "scholar" in scholar-practitioner. *Journal of Student Affairs Research and Practice, 49*(4), 377–396.

Stage, F. K., & Manning, K. (2003). *Research in the college context.* New York: Routledge.

Steedle, J. (2010). On the foundations of standardized assessment of college outcomes and estimating value added. In K. Carey & M. Schneider (Eds.), *Accountability in higher education* (pp. 7–31). New York: Palgrave Macmillan.

Suskie, L. (2004). *Assessing student learning: A common sense guide.* Bolton: Anker.

Suskie, L. (2009). *Assessing student learning: A common sense guide* (2nd ed.). San Francisco: Jossey-Bass.

Suskie, L. (2015). Introduction to measuring co-curricular learning. *New Directions for Institutional Research, 164,* 5–13.

Suskie, L. (2018). *Assessing student learning: A common sense guide* (3rd ed.). San Francisco: Jossey-Bass.

Swing, R. L., & Ross, L. E. (2016a). A new vision for institutional research. *Change: The Magazine of Higher Learning,* 6–13. Retrieved from http://www.airweb.org/resources/irstudies

Swing, R. L., & Ross, L. E. (2016b). *Statement of aspirational practice for institutional research.* Tallahassee, FL: Association for Institutional Research. Retrieved from http://www.airweb.org/aspirationalstatement

Task Force on the Future of Student Affairs. (2010). *Envisioning the future of student affairs.* Washington DC: ACPA & NASPA.

Thomas, G. (2013). *How to do your research project: A guide for students in education and applied social sciences.* London: Sage.

Timm, D. M., Barham, J. D., McKinney, K., & Knerr, A.R. (2013). *Assessment in practice: A companion guide to the ASK Standards.* Washington, DC: ACPA.

Tinto, V. (1993). *Leaving college: Rethinking the causes and cures of student attrition* (2nd ed.). Chicago: University of Chicago Press.

Trochim, W. M., Donnelly, J. P., & Arora, K. (2015). *Research methods: The essential knowledge base* (2nd ed.). Boston: Cengage Learning.

Truth and Reconciliation Commission of Canada. (2015). Truth and Reconciliation Commission of Canada: Calls to action. Retrieved from http://www.trc.ca/websites/trcinstitution/File/2015/Findings/Calls_to_Action_English2.pdf

Tull, A., & Kuk, L. (2012). *New realities in the management of student affairs.* Sterling, VA: Stylus.

Twain, M. (1906). Chapters from my autobiography. *North American Review.* Urbana, IL: Project Gutenberg. Retrieved August 23, 2017 from www.gutenberg.org/ebooks/19987.

U.S. Department of Education (2006). *A test of leadership: Charting the future of U.S. higher education.* Washington, DC: U.S. Department of Education.

Upcraft, M. L. (2003). Assessment and evaluation. In S. R. Komives, D. B. Woodard, & Associates (Eds). *Student services: A handbook for the profession* (pp. 555–572). San Francisco: Jossey-Bass.

Upcraft, M. L., & Schuh, J. H. (1996). *Assessment in student affairs: A guide for practitioners.* San Francisco: Jossey-Bass.

Walvoord, B. E. (2004). *Assessment clear and simple: A practical guide for institutions, departments, and general education.* San Francisco: Jossey-Bass.

Weinbach, R. W., & Grinnell, R. M. (2001). *Statistics for social workers* (5th ed.). Boston: Allyn & Bacon.

Wise, V. L. (2014, June). *Assessment Map*ping.* Program presented at the College Student Educators International Assessment Institute, Denver, CO.

Wise, V. L., & Barham, M. A. (2012). Moving beyond surveys. *About Campus, 17*(2), 26–29. doi:10.1002/abc.21077

Woodard, D. B. Jr., Love, P., & Komives, S. R. (2000). Learning and development. *New Directions for Student Services, 92,* 49–60.

Yarbrough, D. B., Shula, L. M., Hopson, R. K., & Caruthers, F. A. (2010). *The program evaluation standards: A guide for evaluators and evaluation users* (3rd ed.). Thousand Oaks, CA: Corwin Press.

Yousey-Elsener, K. M. (2013). *Successful assessment for student affairs: A how-to guide.* Little Falls, NJ: PaperClip Communications.

Yousey-Elsener, K. M. (2014). *Assessment: Data collection and reporting advanced skills for student affairs.* Little Falls, NJ: PaperClip Communications.

Yousey-Elsner, K. M., Bentrin, E. M., & Henning, G. W. (Eds.). (2015). *Coordinating student affairs divisional assessment: A practical guide.* Sterling, VA: Stylus.

INDEX